The Ultimate Guide to Great Parenting: Tips for Success

Hagen Laura

Published by Hagen Laura, 2024.

While every precaution has been taken in the preparation of this book, the publisher assumes no responsibility for errors or omissions, or for damages resulting from the use of the information contained herein.

THE ULTIMATE GUIDE TO GREAT PARENTING: TIPS FOR SUCCESS

First edition. April 2, 2024.

ISBN: 979-8223257783

Written by Hagen Laura.

Table of Contents

Chapter 1: Introduction

- WHAT IS PARENTING?

Parenting is a complex and multifaceted concept that involves the lifelong process of raising a child and providing them with the necessary physical, emotional, social, and intellectual support to help them grow and develop into responsible and successful individuals. It is a crucial aspect of human development, as parents play a significant role in shaping their children's values, beliefs, attitudes, and behaviors. Parenting is not a one-size-fits-all approach; it requires a combination of love, patience, discipline, and guidance to meet the unique needs and challenges of each child.

One of the key components of parenting is nurturing. Nurturing involves providing a safe, secure, and supportive environment for children to thrive and grow. It encompasses showing love and affection, providing emotional support, and meeting the basic needs of children such as food, shelter, and clothing. Nurturing also involves fostering a strong bond and connection between parents and children, which is crucial for healthy development and building trust and a sense of security in children. Parents who are nurturing create a positive and loving atmosphere in which children can explore, learn, and develop their full potential.

Another important aspect of parenting is discipline. Discipline involves setting boundaries, establishing rules, and enforcing consequences to help children learn right from wrong and develop self-control and responsibility. Discipline is essential for teaching children to make good decisions, solve problems, and respect authority. It also helps children learn how to regulate their emotions and behavior, develop empathy and compassion, and build strong relationships with others. Effective discipline is based on a balanced approach that combines clear expectations, consistent enforcement, and positive reinforcement to encourage good behavior and discourage negative behavior.

Communication is also a vital component of parenting. Effective communication involves listening to children, expressing feelings and thoughts, and providing guidance and support in a clear and respectful manner. Good communication helps parents understand their children's needs, concerns, and perspectives, and helps children feel heard, valued, and understood. It also helps build trust, strengthen relationships, and promote healthy emotional development in children. Communication is a two-way street that requires active listening, empathy, and a willingness to engage in open and honest conversations with children.

Parenting also involves teaching and guiding children to help them develop essential life skills and values. Parents are their children's first teachers and role models, shaping their beliefs, attitudes, and behaviors through their words and actions. Parents play a crucial role in helping children learn important skills such as problem-solving, decision-making, communication, and critical thinking. They also instill values such as honesty, compassion, respect, and responsibility, which are essential for building strong character, integrity, and ethical behavior in children. Teaching and guiding children requires patience, consistency, and a commitment to helping children learn, grow, and succeed. It is a lifelong commitment that involves making sacrifices, facing challenges, and celebrating milestones along the way. Parenting is a shared responsibility that requires cooperation, collaboration, and teamwork between parents, caregivers, and other important adults in children's lives. By understanding the key components of parenting and embracing its values and principles, parents can create a nurturing, supportive, and loving environment in which children can thrive and reach their full potential.

- The Role of a Parent

The role of a parent is one of the most significant and influential responsibilities a person can undertake. Parents play a crucial role in the physical, emotional, and cognitive development of their children. Their influence is profound and enduring, shaping the values, beliefs, and behaviors that their children will carry with them throughout their lives. In this essay, we will explore the multifaceted role of parents and examine the various ways in which they impact their children's growth and development.

Role of a Parent in Child Development:

Parents serve as the primary caregivers and protectors of their children, ensuring their basic needs are met and providing a safe and nurturing environment in which they can thrive. From infancy through adolescence, parents are instrumental in shaping their children's physical, emotional, and cognitive development. They are responsible for meeting their children's basic needs, such as food, shelter, and clothing, as well as providing love, support, and guidance as they navigate the challenges of growing up.

In addition to meeting their children's physical needs, parents also play a crucial role in their emotional development. Children learn about love, trust, and empathy from their parents, who serve as their first and most important role models. The nature of the parent-child relationship has a significant impact on a child's emotional well-being, shaping their self-esteem, sense of security, and ability to form healthy relationships with others. Nurturing a positive and loving relationship with their children is essential for parents to promote their emotional development and help them navigate the complexities of human relationships.

Furthermore, parents play a vital role in their children's cognitive development. From the earliest stages of life, children learn through observation, imitation, and interaction with their parents. Parents serve as their children's first teachers, helping them learn language, acquire knowledge, and develop critical thinking skills. The quality of the parent-child relationship, as well as the level of parental involvement in their children's education, has a direct impact on their academic success and intellectual development. Parents who are actively engaged in their children's learning and provide a stimulating home environment can help foster a lifelong love of learning and set the stage for academic achievement.

Parenting Styles and their Impact on Child Development:

The parenting style a parent employs can have a profound impact on their child's growth and development. Research has identified four primary parenting styles - authoritarian, authoritative, permissive, and uninvolved - each characterized by different levels of parental control, warmth, and responsiveness. Authoritative parenting, which is characterized by high levels of warmth and responsiveness coupled with reasonable levels of control and discipline, has been consistently associated with positive outcomes for children, including higher academic achievement, better social skills, and lower rates of behavioral problems. In contrast, authoritarian parenting, characterized by high levels of control and discipline but low levels of warmth and responsiveness, has been linked to negative outcomes for children, such as lower self-esteem, poor academic performance, and higher rates of anxiety and depression.

The Impact of Parental Involvement and Support:

Parental involvement in a child's life is crucial for their overall well-being and development. Research has shown that children whose parents are actively engaged in their education, extra-curricular activities, and social lives are more likely to succeed academically, have higher self-esteem, and form healthier relationships with others. Parental involvement can take many forms, including attending parent-teacher conferences, volunteering at school events, and participating in their children's hobbies and interests. Additionally, providing emotional support and encouragement can help children develop a sense of confidence and resilience, enabling them to overcome challenges and setbacks.

The Role of Parents in Instilling Values and Beliefs:

Parents serve as the primary moral and ethical guides for their children, helping them develop a sense of right and wrong, empathy, and respect for others. The values and beliefs that parents instill in their children will shape their attitudes, behaviors, and choices throughout their lives. By modeling positive values such as honesty, integrity, and compassion, parents can help cultivate a strong moral compass in their children and foster a sense of social responsibility. Additionally, parents can introduce their children to different cultures, religions, and perspectives, helping them develop a broader worldview and empathy towards others. Parents serve as the primary caregivers, role models, teachers, and moral guides for their children, shaping their physical, emotional, and cognitive development in profound ways. By providing love, support, and guidance, parents can help foster a strong sense of self-worth, resilience, and empathy in their children, enabling them to navigate the challenges of growing up and succeed in life. Parenting is a challenging and rewarding journey that requires patience, dedication, and a deep commitment to the well-being of one's children. By recognizing the importance of their role and actively engaging in the growth and development of their children, parents can make a lasting and positive impact on their lives.

- Importance of Effective Parenting

Effective parenting is a crucial factor in a child's development and overall well-being. It plays a significant role in shaping a child's personality, behavior, and social skills. Research has shown that children who receive effective parenting are more likely to excel academically, have better emotional regulation, and develop positive relationships with others. This highlights the importance of parents taking an active role in their child's upbringing and providing a nurturing and supportive environment.

One of the key aspects of effective parenting is setting boundaries and expectations for children. Children thrive in environments where there are clear rules and guidelines for behavior. By establishing consistent rules and consequences, parents help children understand what is expected of them and how to behave appropriately in different situations. This not only teaches children important values such as responsibility and respect, but also helps them develop self-discipline and self-control.

Communication is another essential aspect of effective parenting. By fostering open and honest communication with their children, parents can build trusting and supportive relationships. This allows children to express their thoughts and feelings, ask for help when needed, and seek guidance from their parents. Good communication also helps parents understand their children's needs and concerns, enabling them to provide the necessary support and guidance.

Moreover, parents play a vital role in providing emotional support and stability for their children. By showing love, empathy, and understanding, parents create a secure attachment with their children, which is crucial for their emotional development. Children who receive emotional support from their parents are more likely to develop a strong sense of self-worth, confidence, and resilience. This helps them navigate challenges and setbacks in life with a positive attitude and a growth mindset.

In addition to emotional support, parents need to provide their children with opportunities for learning and growth. This includes engaging in stimulating and enriching activities that promote cognitive, physical, and social development. By exposing children to a variety of experiences and learning opportunities, parents help them discover their interests, talents, and strengths. This also fosters a love for learning and a curiosity for the world around them, setting them up for success in school and beyond.

Furthermore, effective parenting involves modeling positive behavior and values for children to emulate. Parents serve as role models for their children, shaping their attitudes, beliefs, and behaviors. By demonstrating kindness, respect, honesty, and other positive traits, parents help instill these values in their children. Children learn by observing and imitating their parents, so it is important for parents to lead by example and be mindful of the impact their actions have on their children. By setting boundaries, fostering open communication, providing emotional support, offering learning opportunities, and modeling positive behavior, parents can help their children grow into confident, resilient, and successful individuals. It is important for parents to prioritize their role as caregivers and educators, as the impact of effective parenting lasts a lifetime. Investing time and effort into being an effective parent is not only beneficial for the child, but also for the parent-child relationship and the family as a whole.

Chapter 2: Building a Strong Relationship with Your Child

- COMMUNICATION SKILLS

Communication skills are essential in every aspect of life, whether in personal relationships, professional settings, or academic environments. Effective communication involves not only the ability to convey ideas clearly and coherently but also to listen actively and empathetically to others. In the workplace, good communication skills are crucial for teamwork, problem-solving, conflict resolution, and building strong relationships with colleagues and clients. Moreover, effective communication is a key factor in leadership and management, as it enables managers to provide clear directions, motivate their teams, and create a positive work environment.

One of the fundamental components of communication skills is verbal communication, which includes speaking clearly, using appropriate tone and language, and being able to articulate thoughts and ideas effectively. Verbal communication is crucial in daily interactions, whether in face-to-face conversations, group meetings, or formal presentations. Additionally, non-verbal communication plays a significant role in conveying messages, as body language, facial expressions, and gestures can often communicate more than words. Understanding and being aware of non-verbal cues can help individuals to better interpret others' emotions, intentions, and reactions, leading to more meaningful and effective communication.

Another important aspect of communication skills is written communication, which is essential in professional settings for creating reports, emails, memos, and other written documents. Good writing skills require clarity, conciseness, and organization, as well as an understanding of the audience and purpose of the communication. Moreover, written communication should be free from errors in grammar, punctuation, and spelling to convey professionalism and credibility. Effective writing skills are essential for conveying complex ideas, persuading others, and maintaining clear and accurate records in the workplace.

In addition to verbal and written communication, interpersonal communication skills are crucial for building and maintaining relationships with others. Interpersonal communication involves the ability to listen actively, show empathy and understanding, and engage in constructive dialogue with others. Effective interpersonal communication is essential in resolving conflicts, negotiating agreements, and building trust and rapport with colleagues, clients, and stakeholders. Moreover, interpersonal communication skills are key in developing leadership qualities such as emotional intelligence, conflict resolution, and team building.

Furthermore, communication skills are important in academic settings for conveying ideas, participating in discussions, and presenting research findings. Effective academic communication involves not only the ability to write clearly and persuasively but also to engage in critical thinking, analysis, and synthesis of information. Moreover, academic communication skills include the ability to listen attentively, ask thoughtful questions, and engage in respectful and constructive dialogue with professors and peers. Strong communication skills are crucial for academic success, as they enable students to communicate their thoughts and ideas effectively, participate actively in classroom discussions, and present their research and findings confidently. Effective communication involves verbal and non-verbal communication, written communication, and interpersonal communication skills. Developing strong communication skills can help individuals to build strong relationships, resolve conflicts, lead and manage teams, and succeed in academic and professional pursuits. By improving communication skills, individuals can enhance their ability to convey ideas, build rapport with others, and achieve their personal and professional goals.

- Trust and Respect

Trust and respect are two fundamental components of any healthy relationship, whether it be personal or professional. These two elements are interdependent and crucial for building strong connections with others. Trust is the belief in the reliability, truth, or ability of someone or something, while respect is a feeling of admiration for someone's abilities, qualities, or achievements. Both trust and respect are essential for fostering effective communication, collaboration, and mutual understanding.

In any relationship, trust is the foundation on which everything else is built. Without trust, it is impossible to form a meaningful connection with others. Trust entails relying on someone or something to have your best interests at heart and to act in your best interest. In a professional setting, trust is crucial for creating a supportive work environment where employees feel safe to voice their opinions, share ideas, and take risks. When trust is present, employees are more likely to feel empowered and motivated to contribute to the organization's success.

Respect, on the other hand, is essential for maintaining positive relationships with others. Respect involves recognizing and appreciating the value and worth of others, regardless of their background, opinions, or beliefs. It is about treating others with kindness, dignity, and consideration, regardless of any differences that may exist. In the workplace, respect is essential for creating a harmonious and inclusive environment where employees feel valued, heard, and respected. When employees feel respected, they are more likely to feel motivated, engaged, and committed to their work.

Trust and respect are closely intertwined, as they both involve valuing and appreciating others. Trust is built upon a foundation of mutual respect, as it requires believing in the integrity, abilities, and intentions of others. Likewise, respect is often earned through demonstrating trustworthiness, honesty, and reliability. When trust and respect are present in a relationship, it creates a positive feedback loop that strengthens the bond between individuals and fosters open communication, collaboration, and mutual support.

Building trust and respect in a relationship requires time, effort, and commitment from all parties involved. It involves being honest, transparent, and reliable in your interactions with others. It also requires listening actively, communicating effectively, and demonstrating empathy and understanding. Trust and respect are not one-sided, but rather a two-way street that requires effort from both parties. By consistently demonstrating trust and respect in your interactions with others, you can foster strong, positive relationships that are built on a foundation of mutual trust and respect. They are interdependent and crucial for building strong connections with others. Trust involves relying on someone or something to act in your best interest and is built upon a foundation of mutual respect. Respect involves recognizing and appreciating the value and worth of others and is essential for creating a harmonious and inclusive environment. By fostering trust and respect in your interactions with others, you can create positive, supportive relationships that enhance communication, collaboration, and mutual understanding.

- Quality Time Together

Quality time together refers to the intentional and meaningful interactions that individuals or groups engage in to strengthen their relationships and foster connection. This can take many forms, such as engaging in activities, having conversations, or simply being present with one another. Quality time is essential for building trust, deepening bonds, and creating memories that last a lifetime.

In today's fast-paced world, quality time together is often overlooked or sacrificed in favor of other obligations such as work, school, or personal pursuits. However, research has shown that spending quality time with loved ones has numerous benefits for mental, emotional, and physical well-being. It can reduce stress, improve communication, increase feelings of happiness and fulfillment, and strengthen relationships.

There are many ways to make the most of quality time together. One important factor is to prioritize and schedule time for each other in your busy schedules. Setting aside dedicated time for activities, conversations, or just being in each other's presence can help ensure that you have meaningful interactions without distractions. It is also important to be fully present during these times, putting away phones, turning off the TV, and actively listening and engaging with one another.

Quality time can take many forms, depending on the preferences and interests of the individuals involved. Some may enjoy going on outdoor adventures, such as hiking or camping, while others may prefer cozy nights at home watching movies or playing board games. The key is to find activities that both parties enjoy and that allow for meaningful interaction and connection. It's also important to be open to trying new things and stepping out of your comfort zone to create new experiences and memories together.

Effective communication is a crucial component of quality time together. This involves expressing thoughts and feelings honestly, listening attentively, and being empathetic and supportive. Healthy communication can help resolve conflicts, build trust, and deepen understanding and connection between individuals. It is important to create a safe and open environment for dialogue, where both parties feel comfortable expressing themselves and being vulnerable with one another.

In addition to spending quality time together as a couple or family, it is also important to carve out individual time for self-care and personal growth. Taking care of your own needs and interests can help you show up as your best self in your relationships and bring a sense of balance and fulfillment to your life. This can include pursuing hobbies, engaging in physical activity, or simply taking time to relax and recharge. By prioritizing and making time for meaningful interactions, engaging in activities that foster connection, and practicing effective communication, individuals can strengthen their bonds, create lasting memories, and experience increased happiness and fulfillment in their relationships. Investing in quality time with loved ones is a valuable and rewarding endeavor that can have long-lasting benefits for both parties involved.

Chapter 3: Setting Boundaries and Rules

- CONSISTENCY IS KEY

Consistency is a fundamental principle that underpins success in various aspects of life. Whether it be personal development, professional growth, or academic achievement, maintaining a consistent effort is essential for achieving long-term goals. Consistency involves the dedication to a particular task or goal over a sustained period of time, enabling individuals to make progress gradually and steadily. It is not about achieving perfection or excellence immediately, but rather about making incremental improvements consistently over time. Consistency requires discipline, commitment, and perseverance, as well as the ability to stay focused and motivated despite challenges and setbacks.

In the realm of personal development, consistency plays a crucial role in shaping habits and behaviors that contribute to overall well-being and success. By engaging in activities such as exercise, meditation, reading, or journaling on a regular basis, individuals can cultivate positive habits that support their physical, mental, and emotional health. Consistency helps individuals build momentum and make progress towards their goals, whether they are related to health and fitness, personal growth, or self-improvement. By establishing a consistent routine and sticking to it, individuals can develop resilience, self-discipline, and a sense of accomplishment that boosts their confidence and self-esteem.

Consistency is also paramount in the professional realm, where it is linked to productivity, efficiency, and effectiveness in the workplace. By consistently showing up, meeting deadlines, and delivering high-quality work, employees can build trust, credibility, and a reputation for reliability among their colleagues and superiors. Consistency in performance is often a key factor in determining success in one's career, as it demonstrates dedication, accountability, and a strong work ethic. By setting clear goals, establishing priorities, and organizing tasks efficiently, professionals can streamline their workflow and maximize their productivity, leading to greater job satisfaction and career advancement opportunities.

In the academic sphere, consistency is a cornerstone of success in learning and education. By maintaining a regular study schedule, attending classes consistently, and completing assignments on time, students can improve their academic performance, understanding, and retention of knowledge. Consistency in studying and revising material helps students build a solid foundation of understanding and skills that are essential for academic success. By engaging with course material regularly, participating actively in class discussions, and seeking help when needed, students can deepen their understanding, develop critical thinking skills, and excel academically.

To cultivate consistency in various areas of life, individuals can adopt several strategies and practices that support their long-term goals and aspirations. Setting specific, measurable, achievable, relevant, and time-bound (SMART) goals can help individuals stay focused, motivated, and accountable for their progress. Creating a daily or weekly schedule, prioritizing tasks, and breaking down big goals into smaller, manageable steps can help individuals stay organized and on track. Developing a growth mindset, cultivating self-discipline, and celebrating small wins along the way can boost motivation and sustain momentum towards achieving larger goals. By maintaining a consistent effort, staying focused, and persevering in the face of challenges, individuals can make progress towards their goals gradually and steadily. Consistency helps individuals build positive habits, enhance productivity, and improve performance in various aspects of life. By setting clear goals, establishing routines, and holding themselves accountable for their actions, individuals can cultivate resilience, self-discipline, and a growth mindset that propel them towards success. So, remember, consistency is not about perfection or excellence overnight, but about making incremental improvements consistently over time to reach your full potential.

- Teaching Responsibility

Teaching responsibility is an essential aspect of education that goes beyond merely imparting knowledge and skills. It involves instilling in students a sense of accountability for their actions, decisions, and commitments. By teaching responsibility, educators help prepare students for success both academically and in their future careers. This essay will explore the importance of teaching responsibility in the education system, strategies for incorporating responsibility into the curriculum, and the benefits it offers to students.

One of the key reasons why teaching responsibility is crucial in education is that it helps students develop important life skills that are essential for success in all areas of their lives. Responsibility is a skill that can be applied in various contexts, such as managing time effectively, completing tasks on time, and being accountable for one's actions. Students who are taught to be responsible are better equipped to handle the demands of higher education, the workforce, and their personal relationships. By cultivating a sense of responsibility early on, educators help students build a solid foundation for their future success.

Incorporating responsibility into the curriculum can be done in various ways, depending on the age and developmental stage of the students. At the elementary level, teachers can introduce responsibility through simple tasks such as taking care of classroom supplies, cleaning up after oneself, and following classroom rules. As students progress through middle and high school, they can be given more complex responsibilities, such as managing their time effectively, keeping track of deadlines, and working collaboratively in group projects. By gradually increasing the level of responsibility assigned to students, educators help them develop the skills and mindset needed to succeed in the real world.

One effective strategy for teaching responsibility is to model responsible behavior and attitudes as an educator. Students look up to their teachers as role models, so it is important for educators to demonstrate responsible behavior in their interactions with students, colleagues, and the school community. By showing students what responsibility looks like in action, educators can inspire them to adopt similar habits and attitudes in their own lives. Additionally, educators can incorporate discussions and activities that emphasize the importance of responsibility in their teaching, such as setting goals, managing deadlines, and reflecting on one's actions.

Another important aspect of teaching responsibility is providing students with opportunities to practice and develop this skill in a supportive environment. Educators can design learning experiences that require students to take on responsibilities and face the consequences of their actions in a controlled setting. For example, educators can assign group projects that require students to collaborate and communicate effectively, thereby fostering a sense of accountability among the group members. By providing students with opportunities to practice responsibility in a safe and supportive environment, educators help them develop the confidence and competence needed to handle real-world challenges.

Teaching responsibility offers numerous benefits to students, both in the short term and in the long term. In the short term, students who are taught to be responsible are more likely to exhibit positive behaviors in the classroom, such as completing assignments on time, participating actively in discussions, and respecting their peers and teachers. These behaviors create a positive learning environment that promotes academic success and student engagement. In the long term, students who have developed a strong sense of responsibility are better prepared to navigate the challenges of adulthood, such as balancing work and family obligations, making ethical decisions, and contributing positively to their communities. By teaching responsibility, educators equip students with the skills and mindset needed to thrive in a complex and dynamic world. By incorporating responsibility into the curriculum, educators prepare students for success in higher education, the workforce, and their personal lives. Strategies for teaching responsibility include modeling responsible behavior, providing opportunities for students to practice responsibility, and emphasizing the importance of accountability in teaching. The benefits of teaching responsibility are numerous, including improved academic performance, enhanced student engagement, and better preparation for the challenges of adulthood.

- Understanding Consequences

Understanding consequences is crucial in every aspect of life, as the outcomes of our actions can have a profound impact on ourselves and those around us. Whether it be in personal relationships, professional settings, or societal contexts, being able to anticipate and evaluate the consequences of our decisions is a key skill that can help us make informed choices. By understanding the potential outcomes of our actions, we are better equipped to make decisions that align with our values and goals, and ultimately lead to positive results.

One of the key aspects of understanding consequences is being able to recognize the interconnectedness of our actions and the effects they have on different aspects of our lives. For example, in a professional setting, a decision to prioritize short-term gains over long-term sustainability may lead to negative consequences such as diminished reputation or financial instability. By taking a holistic approach and considering the broader implications of our choices, we can make decisions that are not only beneficial in the short term but also sustainable in the long run.

Furthermore, understanding consequences involves acknowledging the potential ripple effects of our actions on others. Our decisions do not exist in a vacuum and can have a domino effect on those around us. For instance, a careless remark made in a social setting may hurt someone's feelings and strain a relationship. By being mindful of the impact our actions can have on others, we can cultivate empathy and consideration in our interactions, leading to healthier relationships and a more harmonious social environment.

In addition to considering the immediate effects of our actions, understanding consequences also involves recognizing the indirect and long-term implications of our decisions. For example, a choice to neglect self-care and prioritize work over personal well-being may lead to burnout and decreased productivity in the long run. By taking a proactive approach and considering the potential long-term consequences of our actions, we can make choices that promote our overall health and well-being.

Moreover, understanding consequences requires a willingness to take responsibility for our actions and accept the outcomes, whether positive or negative. By owning up to the repercussions of our decisions, we can learn from our mistakes, make amends when necessary, and strive to make better choices in the future. This sense of accountability not only fosters personal growth and development but also builds trust and credibility in our relationships, both professionally and personally. By considering the interconnectedness of our choices, acknowledging the impact on others, and recognizing the long-term implications of our decisions, we can navigate life's complexities with greater clarity and purpose. Ultimately, by cultivating a deeper understanding of consequences, we can strive to make choices that align with our values, enhance our well-being, and contribute to a more positive and fulfilling life.

Chapter 4: Encouraging Positive Behavior

- PRAISE AND ENCOURAGEMENT

Praise and encouragement are essential components in motivating individuals to achieve their fullest potential and excel in their endeavors. Whether in the workplace, classroom, or personal relationships, positive reinforcement plays a critical role in boosting morale, inspiring confidence, and fostering a supportive environment for growth and development. By acknowledging and celebrating efforts, progress, and accomplishments, praise and encouragement can have a profound impact on an individual's self-esteem, motivation, and overall well-being.

One of the key benefits of praise and encouragement is the reinforcement of desired behaviors and actions. When individuals receive positive feedback for their efforts and achievements, they are more likely to continue demonstrating those behaviors in the future. This can lead to increased productivity, improved performance, and a greater sense of satisfaction and fulfillment. By recognizing and acknowledging the hard work and dedication of others, leaders and influencers can create a culture of excellence and continuous improvement within their organizations and communities.

In addition to reinforcing positive behaviors, praise and encouragement also serve to boost confidence and self-esteem. When individuals receive recognition and validation for their contributions and accomplishments, they feel valued and appreciated, which can enhance their sense of self-worth and belief in their abilities. This, in turn, can inspire individuals to take on new challenges, push past their comfort zones, and strive for higher levels of success.

By providing meaningful and genuine praise and encouragement, leaders and mentors can empower others to believe in themselves and reach their full potential.

Furthermore, praise and encouragement have the power to create a supportive and inclusive environment where individuals feel motivated and inspired to work together towards common goals. When people feel recognized, appreciated, and valued for their unique contributions and talents, they are more likely to collaborate effectively, communicate openly, and support one another in their endeavors. This sense of camaraderie and teamwork can lead to increased cohesion, synergy, and overall success within teams and organizations. By fostering a culture of praise and encouragement, leaders and influencers can cultivate a positive and uplifting atmosphere that encourages individuals to thrive and flourish.

It is important to note that praise and encouragement are most effective when they are specific, sincere, and timely. Generic or insincere compliments can come across as disingenuous or manipulative, and may not have the intended impact on the recipient. Instead, it is essential to be genuine and authentic in acknowledging the efforts and achievements of others, highlighting specific details or examples that demonstrate their hard work and dedication. Additionally, providing timely feedback allows individuals to quickly recognize the value of their contributions and adjust their behaviors accordingly, leading to continuous improvement and growth. By recognizing and celebrating the efforts and achievements of others, leaders and influencers can reinforce positive behaviors, boost confidence and self-esteem, foster a supportive and inclusive environment, and drive individuals towards greater success and fulfillment. By incorporating praise and encouragement into our interactions and relationships, we can create a positive and empowering culture that brings out the best in ourselves and others.

- Setting a Good Example

Setting a good example is a crucial aspect of leadership and influence. Whether in the workplace, in our communities, or in our personal lives, the way we conduct ourselves and the choices we make have a significant impact on those around us. By setting a good example, we not only inspire others to follow in our footsteps but also contribute to a positive and productive environment where values such as integrity, accountability, and respect are upheld.

One of the key elements of setting a good example is leading by actions rather than words. People are more likely to be influenced by what they see rather than what they hear. Therefore, it is important for leaders to demonstrate the behavior they expect from others. For example, if a manager expects his team to be punctual and dedicated, he must be the first to arrive at work and show dedication to his tasks. By consistently modeling the desired behaviors, leaders can inspire others to follow suit and create a culture of excellence.

Another important aspect of setting a good example is practicing good communication skills. Effective communication is essential for building trust, resolving conflicts, and fostering collaboration. Leaders who are open, honest, and transparent in their communication can earn the respect and loyalty of their team members. By actively listening to others, providing constructive feedback, and addressing concerns in a timely manner, leaders can create a supportive and inclusive environment where everyone feels heard and valued.

Furthermore, setting a good example involves making ethical decisions and acting with integrity. Ethical leadership is characterized by honesty, fairness, and consistency in one's actions. Leaders who uphold ethical standards and moral values not only inspire trust and loyalty but also set a positive precedent for others to follow. By demonstrating integrity in difficult situations, such as standing up against unethical behavior or admitting mistakes, leaders can build credibility and earn the respect of their peers.

In addition to ethical leadership, setting a good example also requires being mindful of one's attitude and behavior towards others. Treating people with respect, empathy, and kindness is essential for building positive relationships and fostering a sense of community. Leaders who show compassion and understanding towards their colleagues create a supportive and inclusive environment where everyone feels valued and appreciated. By demonstrating empathy and being willing to help others in times of need, leaders can inspire camaraderie and teamwork among their team members.

Lastly, setting a good example involves being a lifelong learner and continuously improving oneself. Leaders who invest in their personal and professional development not only stay ahead of the curve but also inspire others to do the same. By seeking feedback, attending training sessions, and pursuing new opportunities for growth, leaders can show their commitment to excellence and inspire others to strive for continuous improvement. In a rapidly changing world, leaders who embrace change, adapt to new challenges, and embrace innovation can set a positive example for others to follow. By leading by actions, practicing good communication skills, upholding ethical standards, demonstrating empathy, and being a lifelong learner, leaders can inspire others to follow in their footsteps and create a positive and productive environment. In today's complex and fast-paced world, the ability to set a good example is more important than ever. Leaders who embrace their role as role models and show integrity, empathy, and a commitment to excellence can make a significant impact on those around them.

- Discipline with Love

Discipline with love is a concept that involves implementing discipline in a way that is supportive, empathetic, and nurturing towards the individual being disciplined. This approach recognizes that discipline is not simply about punishment or control, but rather about teaching and guiding individuals towards making positive choices and developing important life skills. By combining discipline with love, individuals are able to learn from their mistakes in a safe and caring environment, rather than feeling isolated or disconnected from those who are trying to help them grow.

One of the key principles of discipline with love is the importance of maintaining a strong and positive relationship with the individual being disciplined. This means approaching discipline with empathy and understanding, rather than with anger or frustration. By showing love and compassion towards the individual, disciplinary actions are more likely to be effective and well-received. It is important for individuals to feel supported and cared for, even in moments of correction or guidance. This can help strengthen the bond between the disciplinarian and the individual, and create a more positive and trusting environment for growth and development.

Another important aspect of discipline with love is the need for clear and consistent communication. It is essential for individuals to understand the reasons behind disciplinary actions, and for expectations to be clearly defined. This helps individuals to understand why certain behaviors are not acceptable, and what they can do to improve and grow. By communicating openly and honestly, individuals are more likely to respond positively to discipline, and to see it as an opportunity for personal growth rather than a form of punishment. This kind of transparency and openness can help foster a sense of trust and understanding within the disciplinary relationship.

Discipline with love also involves focusing on teaching and guiding individuals towards better choices and behaviors, rather than simply punishing or controlling them. This means taking the time to listen to the individual, understand their perspective, and work with them to find solutions that are both effective and supportive. Rather than resorting to punitive measures, discipline with love encourages individuals to learn from their mistakes, take responsibility for their actions, and make positive changes moving forward. By focusing on constructive and proactive solutions, individuals are more likely to feel empowered and motivated to make positive changes in their lives.

It is important to remember that discipline with love is not about being permissive or lenient, but rather about finding a balance between setting boundaries and offering support. It is important for individuals to understand that there are consequences for their actions, but that these consequences are meant to help them learn and grow, rather than simply to punish them. By approaching discipline with love and understanding, individuals are more likely to feel motivated to make positive changes, and to see discipline as a valuable tool for personal growth and development. By combining discipline with empathy, understanding, and support, individuals are more likely to respond positively to disciplinary actions, and to see them as opportunities for growth and development. Through clear communication, positive reinforcement, and a focus on teaching and guiding, discipline with love can help individuals learn from their mistakes, take responsibility for their actions, and make positive changes in their lives. By approaching discipline with love and compassion, individuals can develop important life skills, build stronger relationships, and work towards becoming their best selves.

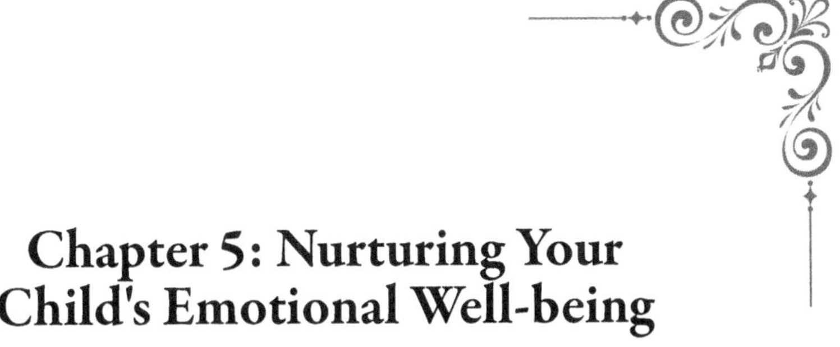

Chapter 5: Nurturing Your Child's Emotional Well-being

- SUPPORTING THEIR FEELINGS

Supporting someone's feelings is an essential aspect of building strong relationships and fostering a sense of emotional well-being. When we support someone's feelings, we show them that we care about their emotional state and are willing to listen and provide validation for their experiences. It involves being empathetic, understanding, and non-judgmental towards the other person's emotions, no matter how they may be feeling. By offering support in this way, we can help the person feel seen, heard, and valued, which can ultimately lead to increased trust and a deeper connection in the relationship.

One of the key ways to support someone's feelings is through active listening. Active listening involves fully focusing on the speaker, understanding their emotions and perspectives, and providing feedback that demonstrates understanding and empathy. This can involve using verbal cues such as nodding, paraphrasing what the person has said, and asking clarifying questions to show that you are engaged and interested in what they have to say. By practicing active listening, you can create a safe and supportive environment for the person to express their feelings and thoughts without fear of judgment or criticism.

Another important aspect of supporting someone's feelings is validation. Validation involves acknowledging and accepting the other person's emotions as valid and understandable, even if you may not agree with them. It is important to remember that feelings are subjective and personal, and each individual has the right to feel their emotions without being told that they are wrong or invalid. By validating someone's feelings, you can help them feel understood and accepted, which can be incredibly validating and comforting in times of distress or difficulty.

In addition to active listening and validation, it is also important to offer practical support to someone in need. This can involve offering help or assistance in a tangible way, such as offering to run errands, cook a meal, or provide a listening ear. By showing up for someone and offering practical support, you can demonstrate that you care about their well-being and are willing to go out of your way to help them in times of need. This can be particularly important for individuals who may be going through a challenging time or facing a difficult situation, as practical support can help alleviate some of the stress and burden they may be feeling.

It is also important to be mindful of your own emotional boundaries when supporting someone's feelings. While it is important to be empathetic and understanding towards the other person's emotions, it is also crucial to prioritize your own emotional well-being and set healthy boundaries in the relationship. This can involve recognizing when you need to take a step back or seek support for yourself, especially if you find yourself feeling overwhelmed or emotionally drained by the other person's emotions. By taking care of your own emotional needs, you can ensure that you are better equipped to support someone else effectively and maintain a healthy balance in the relationship. By practicing active listening, validation, offering practical support, and maintaining healthy emotional boundaries, you can create a safe and supportive environment for the other person to express their emotions and feel understood and valued. Remember that feelings are subjective and personal, and each individual has the right to feel their emotions without judgment or criticism. By offering your empathy, understanding, and care, you can help someone feel supported and connected, ultimately strengthening your relationship and creating a sense of emotional well-being for both parties.

- Teaching Emotional Intelligence

Teaching emotional intelligence is a crucial aspect of education that has gained significant attention in recent years. Emotional intelligence, often referred to as EQ, is the ability to understand, manage, and express one's own emotions effectively, as well as the ability to recognize and respond to the emotions of others. Research has shown that individuals with high emotional intelligence tend to have better mental health, stronger relationships, and higher levels of success in both personal and professional settings.

One of the key components of teaching emotional intelligence is helping students develop self-awareness. Self-awareness involves recognizing and understanding one's own emotions, as well as the impact that those emotions have on behavior and decision-making. By helping students become more self-aware, educators can empower them to better regulate their emotions and make more thoughtful choices in their interactions with others.

Another important aspect of teaching emotional intelligence is supporting students in developing social awareness. Social awareness involves the ability to recognize and understand the emotions of others, as well as the ability to adapt one's behavior to different social situations. By helping students develop social awareness, educators can encourage them to be more empathetic, compassionate, and inclusive in their interactions with peers. This can lead to stronger relationships, improved communication skills, and a greater sense of connectedness within the school community.

In addition to self-awareness and social awareness, teaching emotional intelligence also involves helping students develop emotional regulation skills. Emotional regulation involves the ability to manage and control one's emotions in a healthy and constructive way. By teaching students strategies for regulating their emotions, educators can help them avoid impulsive or reactive behavior and instead respond thoughtfully and rationally to challenging situations. This can lead to improved self-control, better decision-making, and reduced stress and anxiety.

Furthermore, teaching emotional intelligence can also involve helping students develop relationship management skills. Relationship management involves the ability to build and maintain positive relationships with others, as well as the ability to resolve conflicts and communicate effectively. By teaching students how to navigate the complexities of interpersonal relationships, educators can empower them to be more successful in their personal and professional lives. By helping students develop self-awareness, social awareness, emotional regulation, and relationship management skills, educators can empower them to navigate the complex world of emotions with confidence and resilience. By integrating emotional intelligence into the curriculum, educators can help prepare students for success in school, work, and life.

- Handling Emotional Outbursts

Handling emotional outbursts is an important skill that is essential in maintaining healthy relationships, both in personal and professional settings. Emotional outbursts can be triggered by a variety of factors, including stress, frustration, and underlying emotional issues. It is important to understand that everyone experiences emotions differently, and what may seem like a minor issue to one person can be a major trigger for another. In order to effectively handle emotional outbursts, it is crucial to approach the situation with empathy, understanding, and patience.

One of the first steps in handling emotional outbursts is to recognize the signs that someone is becoming overwhelmed or upset. These signs can vary from person to person, but common indicators include raised voice, clenched fists, pacing, and rapid breathing. It is important to pay attention to these cues and intervene before the situation escalates further. By being proactive and addressing the issue early on, you can help prevent a full-blown emotional outburst from occurring.

When faced with someone experiencing an emotional outburst, it is important to remain calm and composed. Reacting with anger or frustration will only escalate the situation further and can make the individual feel even more overwhelmed. Instead, take a deep breath and approach the person with a calm and gentle demeanor. Let them know that you are there to support them and that you are willing to listen to what they have to say. By showing empathy and understanding, you can help the individual feel heard and validated, which can go a long way in de-escalating the situation.

As the person begins to express their emotions, it is important to actively listen to what they are saying. Avoid interrupting or offering unsolicited advice, as this can come across as dismissive and make the individual feel invalidated. Instead, listen attentively and validate their feelings by acknowledging their emotions and expressing empathy. Reflect back what they are saying to ensure that you have understood their perspective, and ask open-ended questions to encourage them to share more about what is bothering them. By actively listening and showing genuine interest in the person's feelings, you can help them feel heard and supported.

In some cases, the individual may need time and space to process their emotions before they are ready to talk about what is bothering them. If this is the case, it is important to respect their boundaries and give them the space they need to calm down. Encourage them to take deep breaths, go for a walk, or engage in any other self-soothing activities that help them manage their emotions. Let them know that you are there for them whenever they are ready to talk, and follow up with them at a later time to check in on how they are feeling.

In situations where the emotional outburst is disruptive or harmful, it may be necessary to intervene more assertively to ensure the safety of everyone involved. If the individual is becoming physically aggressive or is putting themselves or others at risk, it is important to take immediate action to de-escalate the situation. This may involve calmly but firmly setting boundaries, removing the individual from the situation, or involving additional support such as a mental health professional or crisis intervention team. It is important to prioritize safety and wellbeing in these situations, and to seek help if needed to ensure that the individual receives the support they require.

After the emotional outburst has subsided, it is important to follow up with the individual to address any underlying issues that may have contributed to the outburst. This can involve having a calm and constructive conversation about what triggered the outburst, how it can be prevented in the future, and what support the individual may need moving forward. By addressing the root causes of the outburst and working together to come up with solutions, you can strengthen your relationship with the individual and build trust and understanding. By being proactive in recognizing the signs of emotional distress, remaining calm and composed during the outburst, actively listening to the individual's feelings, respecting their boundaries, intervening assertively when necessary, and following up with them afterwards, you can effectively manage and de-escalate emotional outbursts in a professional and supportive manner. Remember that everyone experiences emotions differently, and by approaching the situation with compassion and patience, you can help the individual feel heard, validated, and supported during their time of need.

Chapter 6: Fostering Independence and Self-confidence

- ENCOURAGING INDEPENDENCE

Encouraging independence is a crucial aspect of development in individuals of all ages. Independence allows individuals to make decisions, take responsibility for their actions, and develop valuable life skills. It is important for parents, educators, and caregivers to foster independence in children from a young age, as it sets the foundation for self-reliance and success in adulthood. By encouraging independence, individuals can build confidence, problem-solving skills, and a sense of accomplishment.

One way to encourage independence in children is to provide them with opportunities to make choices and take on responsibilities. Giving children the freedom to make decisions, such as choosing their own clothes or deciding what activities to participate in, helps them develop critical thinking skills and a sense of autonomy. Additionally, assigning age-appropriate chores and tasks can teach children the importance of contributing to the household and help them develop valuable life skills.

It is important for parents and caregivers to resist the urge to constantly step in and help children with tasks that they are capable of completing on their own. By allowing children to struggle and learn from their mistakes, parents can help build resilience and strength in their children. It is natural for parents to want to protect their children from failure, but it is through failure that individuals learn valuable lessons and develop essential problem-solving skills.

In addition to providing opportunities for children to make choices and take on responsibilities, it is important for parents, educators, and caregivers to praise and encourage independent behavior. Positive reinforcement is a powerful tool in shaping behavior, and by acknowledging and praising a child's efforts towards independence, adults can motivate children to continue seeking out opportunities to assert their autonomy. Encouraging independence in children can also help foster a sense of self-worth and confidence.

Encouraging independence in adolescents is equally important, as teenagers navigate the transition to adulthood and begin to establish their identity and place in the world. Adolescents who are encouraged to make their own decisions and take on responsibilities are more likely to develop a strong sense of self and be better equipped to handle the challenges that come with growing up. By supporting and empowering teenagers to make informed choices and take ownership of their actions, adults can help them develop essential life skills and build a solid foundation for their future.

In the academic setting, educators play a crucial role in encouraging independence in students. By providing students with opportunities to work independently, set goals, and solve problems on their own, educators can help students develop critical thinking skills and a sense of self-efficacy. It is important for educators to create a supportive and nurturing environment where students feel empowered to take risks and learn from their mistakes. Encouraging independence in students can also help foster a sense of ownership and responsibility for their own learning. By providing opportunities for children to make choices, take on responsibilities, and learn from their mistakes, parents, educators, and caregivers can help individuals develop essential skills and qualities that will serve them well throughout their lives. Independence is not only important for personal growth and development but also for creating a sense of autonomy and self-worth. By fostering independence in children, adolescents, and students, adults can empower individuals to reach their full potential and lead fulfilling lives.

- Building Self-esteem

Building self-esteem is a multifaceted process that has a significant impact on an individual's overall well-being and success in various aspects of life. Self-esteem is defined as a person's overall subjective evaluation of their own worth and value, and it plays a crucial role in shaping one's thoughts, feelings, and behaviors. When individuals have healthy self-esteem, they are more likely to feel confident in their abilities, make positive choices, and maintain positive relationships with others.

There are several key factors that contribute to the development of self-esteem. One of the primary factors is early childhood experiences, including the quality of the relationship with caregivers and the level of support and validation received during formative years. Children who grow up in environments where they feel loved, accepted, and encouraged are more likely to develop a positive sense of self-worth. Conversely, children who experience neglect, abuse, or criticism may struggle with low self-esteem.

Another important factor that influences self-esteem is personal achievements and accomplishments. When individuals set and achieve goals, they experience a sense of mastery and competence that boosts their self-esteem. It is important for individuals to set realistic and attainable goals, as unrealistic expectations can lead to feelings of failure and inadequacy. Celebrating small victories and acknowledging progress can also help to build self-esteem over time.

Social relationships play a significant role in shaping self-esteem as well. Positive relationships with friends, family members, and colleagues can provide support, validation, and a sense of belonging that enhance self-esteem. Conversely, negative or toxic relationships can erode self-esteem and contribute to feelings of worthlessness and self-doubt. It is important for individuals to cultivate healthy relationships and set boundaries with those who undermine their self-worth.

Self-perception and self-talk also play a critical role in shaping self-esteem. Individuals who engage in positive self-talk and have a realistic view of their strengths and weaknesses are more likely to have healthy self-esteem. On the other hand, individuals who engage in negative self-talk, such as self-criticism and self-doubt, are at a higher risk of developing low self-esteem. It is important for individuals to challenge negative beliefs and replace them with more positive and realistic thoughts.

There are several strategies that individuals can use to build and maintain healthy self-esteem. One of the most important strategies is to practice self-care and prioritize one's physical, emotional, and mental well-being. Taking care of oneself through regular exercise, healthy eating, adequate sleep, and stress management can help individuals feel better about themselves and boost their self-esteem. Additionally, engaging in activities that bring joy and fulfillment, such as hobbies, interests, and passions, can also enhance self-esteem.

Another key strategy for building self-esteem is to cultivate a growth mindset. A growth mindset is the belief that one's abilities and intelligence can be developed through effort, perseverance, and learning. Individuals with a growth mindset are more likely to embrace challenges, learn from failure, and persist in the face of setbacks. By adopting a growth mindset, individuals can develop resilience, confidence, and a sense of self-efficacy that strengthens their self-esteem.

Developing self-awareness and self-compassion is also essential for building self-esteem. Self-awareness involves recognizing one's thoughts, feelings, and behaviors without judgment or criticism. By becoming more self-aware, individuals can identify negative patterns of thinking and behavior that undermine their self-esteem and make positive changes to improve their self-perception. Similarly, self-compassion involves treating oneself with kindness, understanding, and acceptance, especially in moments of failure or difficulty. By cultivating self-compassion, individuals can foster a sense of inner worthiness and self-acceptance that bolsters their self-esteem. By understanding the factors that contribute to self-esteem, setting achievable goals, cultivating healthy relationships, challenging negative beliefs, prioritizing self-care, adopting a growth mindset, and practicing self-awareness and self-compassion, individuals can enhance their sense of self-worth and live more fulfilling lives. Ultimately, healthy self-esteem is the foundation for a positive self-concept, resilience, and success in all aspects of life.

- Helping Your Child Find Their Strengths

It is essential for parents to actively support and encourage their children in the process of discovering their unique strengths and talents. By fostering a positive and nurturing environment, parents can help their children build self-confidence, develop a sense of purpose, and achieve their full potential. In this article, we will explore effective strategies and techniques that parents can use to assist their children in identifying and cultivating their strengths.

One of the first steps in helping your child find their strengths is to observe their interests and aptitudes. Pay attention to what activities they gravitate towards and excel in, whether it be sports, arts, academics, or any other realm. Encourage them to explore a wide range of hobbies and extracurricular activities to help them discover areas in which they excel. By providing opportunities for your child to try new things and engage in different experiences, you can help them uncover their natural talents and passions.

Furthermore, it is important for parents to provide positive reinforcement and constructive feedback to their children. Recognizing and praising their efforts, accomplishments, and progress can boost their self-esteem and motivate them to continue exploring and developing their strengths. Encourage your child to set realistic and achievable goals for themselves and celebrate their successes, no matter how big or small. Additionally, offer constructive criticism when necessary, but always in a supportive and non-judgmental manner. This will help your child learn from their mistakes and grow as individuals.

In addition to providing encouragement and support, parents can also help their children develop a growth mindset. Teach them the importance of perseverance, resilience, and continuous learning. Encourage them to embrace challenges, overcome obstacles, and view failures as opportunities for growth and improvement. By instilling a positive attitude towards learning and personal development, parents can help their children build the confidence and determination needed to succeed in any endeavor.

Another effective way to help your child find their strengths is to involve them in goal-setting and self-reflection activities. Encourage them to identify their strengths, weaknesses, interests, and values, and to set goals that align with their aspirations and aspirations. Guide them in developing a plan of action to reach their goals and hold them accountable for their progress. Encourage them to regularly reflect on their achievements and challenges, and to adjust their strategies and approaches accordingly. By involving your child in the goal-setting and self-reflection process, you can empower them to take ownership of their personal development and growth.

Furthermore, parents can help their children find their strengths by providing opportunities for them to showcase and hone their talents. Encourage your child to participate in competitions, performances, exhibitions, or other events that allow them to demonstrate their skills and abilities. Support them in pursuing advanced training, mentorship, or other resources that can help them further develop their strengths. By creating a supportive environment that values and promotes their talents, parents can help their children build confidence, self-esteem, and a sense of purpose in life. By observing their interests, providing positive reinforcement, fostering a growth mindset, involving them in goal-setting and self-reflection activities, and creating opportunities for them to showcase and hone their talents, parents can assist their children in discovering and developing their unique gifts. By instilling a sense of self-awareness, achievement, and purpose in their children, parents can empower them to pursue their passions, overcome challenges, and achieve their full potential. Ultimately, by guiding and supporting their children on their journey of self-discovery and personal growth, parents can help them become confident, resilient, and successful individuals.

Chapter 7: Understanding and Supporting Your Child's Development

- MILESTONES TO LOOK For

When it comes to tracking the developmental progress of young children, there are several key milestones that parents and caregivers should look for. These milestones can provide valuable insights into a child's physical, cognitive, social, and emotional development. By understanding what to expect at various ages and stages of development, parents can better support their child's growth and address any concerns that may arise.

One of the first milestones that parents should be aware of is the development of fine motor skills. Fine motor skills refer to the ability to control and coordinate small muscles in the hands and fingers. In infants, this can be seen in their ability to grasp objects, reach for toys, and eventually feed themselves. As children grow older, they will continue to refine their fine motor skills, such as learning to button clothes, tie shoelaces, and write with a pencil. If a child is struggling with fine motor skills, it may be worth seeking out occupational therapy or other interventions to support their development.

Another important milestone to look for is language development. From the very beginning, babies are communicating with their caregivers through crying, cooing, and eventually babbling. As they grow, children will start to say their first words, string together simple sentences, and eventually engage in more complex conversations. Parents should pay attention to their child's language development and seek out support if they have concerns about speech delays or difficulties. Early intervention can make a significant difference in a child's ability to communicate effectively.

Cognitive milestones are also crucial indicators of a child's development. Cognitive development refers to a child's ability to think, reason, problem-solve, and understand the world around them. From early on, children are constantly learning and exploring their environment, developing memory, attention, and problem-solving skills. As children grow, they will start to engage in more complex cognitive tasks, such as sorting objects by size, shape, or color, and understanding cause and effect relationships. Parents can support their child's cognitive development by providing opportunities for play, exploration, and learning through books, puzzles, and other educational activities.

Social and emotional milestones are equally important to monitor in young children. Social development refers to a child's ability to interact with others, form relationships, and regulate their emotions. From the earliest stages, babies are learning to bond with their caregivers, make eye contact, and respond to social cues. As children grow older, they will start to engage in more social interactions with peers, develop empathy and understanding of others' emotions, and learn to regulate their own emotions and behavior. Parents can support their child's social and emotional development by modeling positive social skills, teaching emotional regulation strategies, and providing opportunities for social interaction.

In brief, physical milestones such as gross motor skills are key indicators of a child's overall development. Gross motor skills refer to a child's ability to control large muscle groups for activities like walking, running, jumping, and climbing. In infants, this may be seen in their ability to lift their head, roll over, and eventually crawl and walk. As children grow older, they will continue to develop their gross motor skills through activities like riding a bike, playing sports, and engaging in physical exercise. Parents can support their child's physical development by encouraging outdoor play, providing opportunities for movement and exercise, and seeking out physical therapy or other interventions if there are concerns about delays or difficulties in this area. By looking for key indicators of fine motor skills, language development, cognitive abilities, social and emotional skills, and physical development, parents and caregivers can better support their child's overall well-being. Early intervention and support can make a significant difference in a child's ability to reach their full potential and thrive in all areas of their development. By understanding what to look for and when to seek help, parents can feel empowered to support their child's growth and development in a positive and proactive way.

- Age-Appropriate Activities

Engaging in age-appropriate activities is essential for promoting the healthy development of children and adolescents. These activities should be tailored to the individual's cognitive, physical, and emotional abilities, ensuring that they are both challenging and achievable. By providing children with opportunities to participate in activities that are suited to their age and level of development, parents and educators can help them build important skills and competencies that will set the foundation for success in later years.

For young children, age-appropriate activities often focus on sensory experiences and exploration. Infants and toddlers may benefit from activities that stimulate their senses, such as playing with different textures, colors, and sounds. These activities can help children develop their motor skills, hand-eye coordination, and language abilities. As children grow older, activities can become more complex and structured, incorporating elements of pretend play, problem-solving, and creativity.

School-age children can benefit from a wide variety of age-appropriate activities that promote social, emotional, and cognitive development. These may include group games, sports, arts and crafts, and educational projects. By participating in these activities, children can learn important skills such as teamwork, communication, and critical thinking. They can also develop their creativity, self-esteem, and sense of accomplishment. These activities can also help children build friendships and social connections, which are important for their emotional well-being.

Adolescents have unique developmental needs that should be taken into account when planning age-appropriate activities. Activities for teenagers should challenge them intellectually and emotionally, while also giving them opportunities for self-expression and independence. Adolescents may benefit from activities such as community service projects, leadership roles in school organizations, and creative pursuits such as writing, music, or art. These activities can help teenagers develop their sense of identity, values, and goals for the future.

It is important for parents and educators to be mindful of the individual needs and interests of each child when planning age-appropriate activities. What may be appropriate for one child may not be suitable for another, so it is important to consider each child's unique strengths, challenges, and preferences. By taking the time to get to know each child and their developmental stage, adults can provide them with opportunities to grow and thrive in a supportive and nurturing environment.

In addition to providing children with age-appropriate activities, it is also important to consider the context in which these activities take place. Children benefit most from activities that are carried out in a safe, structured, and supportive environment. Adults should provide supervision, guidance, and encouragement to help children make the most of their experiences. By creating a positive and inclusive atmosphere, adults can help children feel valued and capable, boosting their self-confidence and motivation to learn and grow. By providing children with opportunities to engage in activities that are suited to their age and level of development, parents and educators can help them build important skills, competencies, and social connections that will serve them well in later years. By being attentive to the unique needs and interests of each child, adults can create a supportive and engaging environment that fosters growth, learning, and well-being. Together, we can help children reach their full potential and lead fulfilling lives.

- Providing a Stimulating Environment

Providing a stimulating environment is essential for promoting learning, creativity, and productivity in various settings, including schools, workplaces, and homes. A stimulating environment is one that encourages curiosity, exploration, and engagement, and it can have a significant impact on an individual's cognitive development, emotional well-being, and overall satisfaction. In this essay, we will explore the key elements of a stimulating environment, the benefits of creating such an environment, and practical strategies for designing and maintaining a stimulating environment in different contexts.

One of the fundamental elements of a stimulating environment is variety. Offering a diverse range of stimuli, such as different colors, textures, sounds, and materials, can help capture and maintain individuals' interest and attention. For example, in a classroom setting, teachers can incorporate a variety of teaching methods, materials, and activities to cater to different learning styles and engage students with varying interests and preferences. Similarly, in a workplace, providing employees with opportunities to work on different projects, collaborate with diverse teams, and participate in various training and development programs can help create a dynamic and stimulating work environment.

Another key element of a stimulating environment is autonomy. Allowing individuals to have a sense of control and ownership over their environment can foster a sense of empowerment, creativity, and agency. For example, in a home setting, parents can involve children in decision-making processes, such as choosing the color of their bedroom walls or selecting their own toys and games, to promote a sense of autonomy and independence. In a workplace, giving employees the freedom to organize their workspace, set their own goals, and make decisions about how they work can help increase motivation, satisfaction, and productivity.

Furthermore, a stimulating environment should be conducive to exploration and discovery. Providing opportunities for individuals to experiment, take risks, and learn from their successes and failures can help foster a growth mindset and a sense of resilience. In educational settings, teachers can encourage students to ask questions, conduct experiments, and engage in hands-on activities to promote critical thinking, problem-solving skills, and a passion for learning. In the workplace, managers can create a culture that values innovation, experimentation, and continuous learning, which can help employees adapt to change, embrace challenges, and develop new skills.

In addition, a stimulating environment should promote social interaction and collaboration. Humans are social beings, and interactions with others play a crucial role in shaping our thinking, behavior, and emotions. In educational settings, encouraging students to work in groups, participate in discussions, and engage in team projects can help develop their communication skills, empathy, and ability to work effectively with others. In the workplace, fostering a culture of collaboration, open communication, and mutual support can enhance teamwork, creativity, and problem-solving capabilities.

Moreover, a stimulating environment should be safe and supportive. Individuals need to feel physically and emotionally secure in their environment to fully engage in learning, exploration, and creativity. Creating a safe and supportive environment involves establishing clear rules and boundaries, providing adequate resources and support, and fostering a sense of belonging and connection. In schools, teachers can create a positive and inclusive classroom atmosphere by promoting respect, empathy, and cooperation among students. In the workplace, managers can implement policies and practices that prioritize employee well-being, work-life balance, and mental health support to create a supportive and healthy work environment. By incorporating elements such as variety, autonomy, exploration, collaboration, and support, individuals can thrive and reach their full potential. Whether in schools, workplaces, or homes, creating a stimulating environment can have a profound impact on individuals' cognitive development, emotional well-being, and overall satisfaction. By understanding the key elements of a stimulating environment and implementing practical strategies to design and maintain such an environment, we can create spaces that inspire and empower individuals to learn, grow, and succeed.

Chapter 8: Handling Challenges and Difficult Situations

- DEALING WITH TANTRUMS

Tantrums are a common occurrence among children, especially those in the toddler or preschool age range. They can be challenging for parents and caregivers to handle, but it is important to address them in a calm and effective manner. Tantrums are a normal part of child development and are typically a result of frustration, exhaustion, hunger, or feeling overwhelmed. Understanding the underlying causes of tantrums can help parents and caregivers respond appropriately and help children learn to manage their emotions in a healthy way.

One key aspect of dealing with tantrums is to remain calm and composed when they occur. It can be difficult to stay calm when a child is screaming or throwing a tantrum, but responding with anger or frustration will only escalate the situation. Taking a deep breath and reminding yourself that tantrums are a normal part of childhood can help you stay grounded and respond in a more effective way. It is important to remember that children are still learning how to regulate their emotions and may not have the skills to express themselves in a healthy way.

It is also important to set limits and boundaries with your child when they are in the midst of a tantrum. While it is tempting to give in to your child's demands to stop the tantrum, this can reinforce the behavior and make it more likely to happen again in the future. Instead, set clear and consistent boundaries with your child and stick to them, even when they are upset. This will teach your child that tantrums are not an effective way to get what they want and help them learn to manage their emotions in a more appropriate way.

Another strategy for dealing with tantrums is to validate your child's feelings while also setting limits on their behavior. It is important to acknowledge your child's emotions and let them know that it is okay to feel upset or frustrated. However, it is also important to make it clear that their behavior is not acceptable and that there are consequences for their actions. By validating your child's feelings and setting limits on their behavior, you can help them learn to express themselves in a healthy way and develop the skills they need to regulate their emotions.

In addition to setting limits and boundaries, it is important to provide your child with tools and techniques to help them manage their emotions in a healthy way. This can include teaching your child deep breathing exercises, using a calm-down corner or space, or engaging in soothing activities like reading a book or drawing. By providing your child with strategies to manage their emotions, you can help them develop the skills they need to navigate difficult situations and regulate their emotions effectively.

It is also important to be consistent in your approach to dealing with tantrums. Children thrive on predictability and routine, so it is important to respond to tantrums in a consistent and predictable manner. This can help your child understand what is expected of them and how to manage their emotions in a healthy way. By responding to tantrums consistently, you can help your child learn to regulate their emotions and develop the skills they need to navigate challenging situations. Understanding the underlying causes of tantrums, setting limits and boundaries, validating your child's feelings, providing tools and techniques to manage emotions, and being consistent in your approach can help you navigate tantrums in a healthy way. By responding to tantrums in a positive and proactive manner, you can help your child learn to regulate their emotions and develop the skills they need to navigate challenging situations.

- Conflict Resolution

Conflict resolution is a crucial facet of interpersonal communication and organizational management. It is the process of addressing disputes or disagreements between individuals or groups in a constructive and mutually beneficial manner. Conflict is an inevitable part of human interaction, and how it is managed can have a significant impact on relationships, productivity, and overall well-being. Effective conflict resolution skills are essential for leaders, managers, and employees at all levels of an organization.

There are various approaches to conflict resolution, each with its own strengths and weaknesses. One common approach is the win-lose model, in which one party prevails over the other. This approach may be effective for resolving simple disputes quickly, but it can damage relationships and lead to resentment. Another approach is the lose-lose model, in which both parties make concessions to reach a compromise. While this approach can maintain harmony in the short term, it may not address the underlying issues causing the conflict.

A more effective approach to conflict resolution is the win-win model, also known as collaborative problem-solving. In this approach, the focus is on finding solutions that satisfy the needs and interests of all parties involved. This requires open communication, active listening, and a willingness to explore different perspectives. Collaborative problem-solving can lead to creative solutions that address the root causes of the conflict and strengthen relationships.

One key aspect of conflict resolution is emotional intelligence, which is the ability to recognize and manage one's own emotions and empathize with others. Emotionally intelligent individuals are better equipped to navigate conflicts, as they can remain calm under pressure, communicate effectively, and build rapport with others. By understanding their own emotions and the emotions of others, individuals can de-escalate conflicts, foster understanding, and find common ground.

Communication is another essential component of conflict resolution. Effective communication involves listening actively, expressing oneself clearly, and seeking to understand the perspectives of others. By communicating openly and honestly, individuals can clarify misunderstandings, address concerns, and work toward mutually acceptable solutions. Additionally, nonverbal communication such as body language, tone of voice, and facial expressions can convey important messages during the conflict resolution process.

Conflict resolution also requires a commitment to fairness and impartiality. Individuals involved in a conflict should strive to be objective, avoid taking sides, and uphold ethical standards. By treating all parties with respect and dignity, individuals can create a safe and supportive environment for resolving disputes. This commitment to fairness can help build trust, foster cooperation, and promote positive outcomes for all involved. By understanding different approaches to conflict resolution, developing emotional intelligence, honing communication skills, and upholding principles of fairness, individuals can effectively manage conflicts and build stronger relationships. With a collaborative mindset and a commitment to constructive problem-solving, individuals can transform conflicts into opportunities for growth, learning, and positive change.

- Coping with Stress

Coping with stress is a topic that is relevant to everyone at some point in their lives. Stress is a natural response to challenging or threatening situations, and it can manifest in a variety of ways, both mentally and physically. In order to effectively cope with stress, it is important to understand its causes and how it impacts our overall well-being. By developing healthy coping mechanisms and strategies, individuals can improve their resilience and ability to manage stress in a positive way.

One common cause of stress is the feeling of being overwhelmed by responsibilities or demands. This can come from work, school, relationships, or other areas of life. When these pressures become too much to handle, it can lead to feelings of anxiety, frustration, and fatigue. In order to cope with this type of stress, it is important to prioritize tasks, set realistic goals, and learn to say no when necessary. By establishing boundaries and taking breaks when needed, individuals can avoid becoming overwhelmed and reduce their overall stress levels.

Another common source of stress is interpersonal conflicts or challenges. Relationships with family members, friends, or coworkers can be both rewarding and challenging, and disagreements or misunderstandings can lead to stress and tension. In order to cope with these types of stressors, it is important to communicate openly and honestly with others, set boundaries and expectations, and seek support when needed. By addressing conflicts head-on and working towards resolution, individuals can strengthen their relationships and reduce the negative impact of stress on their well-being.

In addition to external stressors, internal factors such as perfectionism, self-criticism, and negative thinking can also contribute to feelings of stress. Individuals who are hard on themselves or have unrealistic expectations may find themselves feeling overwhelmed and anxious. In order to cope with this type of stress, it is important to practice self-compassion, challenge negative thoughts, and focus on gratitude and positivity. By cultivating a mindset of self-acceptance and resiliency, individuals can build emotional strength and reduce the impact of internal stressors on their overall well-being.

Physical health and self-care are also important aspects of coping with stress. When individuals are under a lot of stress, they may neglect their physical health, leading to symptoms such as fatigue, headaches, or digestive issues. In order to cope with stress in a healthy way, it is important to prioritize self-care practices such as exercise, healthy eating, adequate sleep, and relaxation techniques. By taking care of their physical health, individuals can improve their resilience to stress and increase their overall well-being. By understanding the causes and impacts of stress, individuals can develop effective ways to manage and reduce their stress levels. By prioritizing self-care, communication, and self-compassion, individuals can improve their resilience and well-being in the face of challenging situations. Ultimately, by taking proactive steps to cope with stress in a positive way, individuals can improve their quality of life and overall happiness.

Chapter 9: Building a Support System

- CONNECTING WITH OTHER Parents

Connecting with other parents can be an invaluable resource for navigating the ups and downs of parenthood. Whether you're a first-time parent looking for advice on sleep training or a seasoned parent seeking camaraderie in the challenges of raising teenagers, building a network of fellow parents can provide support, validation, and a sense of community. In today's fast-paced world, finding time to connect with other parents can be a challenge, but the benefits far outweigh the effort it takes to make those connections. From playdates to parent support groups, there are countless ways to connect with other parents and create a strong support system to lean on when times get tough.

One of the most common ways parents connect with each other is through playdates. These informal gatherings provide an opportunity for children to socialize and play together while parents can chat and build relationships. Playdates can be as simple as meeting at a local park or play area, or as elaborate as hosting a themed playdate at someone's home. Regardless of the setting, playdates offer a chance for parents to bond over their shared experiences of raising children and can lead to lasting friendships for both parents and children alike.

In addition to playdates, parent support groups can be a valuable resource for connecting with other parents and finding a sense of community. These groups are often organized around specific topics or age ranges, such as breastfeeding support groups, single parent groups, or groups for parents of children with special needs. By joining a support group, parents can find a safe space to share their struggles and successes, receive advice and guidance from fellow parents, and feel less alone in their parenting journey. Support groups can also provide access to resources and information that can help parents navigate challenging situations and make informed decisions about their children's health and well-being.

Another way parents can connect with each other is through online communities and social media networks. Platforms like Facebook, Instagram, and parenting forums offer a convenient way for parents to connect and share information, tips, and resources with each other. These online communities can be especially helpful for parents who may not have local support or who have limited time to attend in-person gatherings. By participating in online discussions, parents can build relationships with others who share their interests and concerns, and access a wealth of knowledge and support from a diverse group of parents around the world. Whether through playdates, parent support groups, or online communities, parents can find the encouragement, advice, and friendship they need to navigate the ups and downs of raising children. By making the effort to reach out and connect with other parents, parents can create a network of support that will help them through the joys and struggles of parenting. So, next time you're feeling overwhelmed or isolated in your parenting journey, remember that you're not alone – there are other parents out there who are eager to connect and support you on your parenting journey.

- Seeking Professional Help When Needed

Seeking professional help when needed is an important step in taking care of one's mental health and well-being. In today's fast-paced and stressful world, it is common for individuals to experience difficulties in coping with the demands and pressures of daily life. Whether it be anxiety, depression, relationship issues, or any other mental health concern, seeking help from a qualified professional can make a significant difference in one's quality of life.

Professional help can come in many forms, such as therapy, counseling, medication management, or a combination of these approaches. Therapy, in particular, is a widely used form of treatment that involves talking to a trained mental health professional about your thoughts, feelings, and behaviors.

Through therapy, individuals can gain insight into their problems, learn new coping skills, and develop a better understanding of themselves and their relationships.

When considering seeking professional help, it is important to choose a therapist or counselor who is qualified, experienced, and licensed in their respective field. This ensures that you are receiving the highest quality of care and support tailored to your specific needs. Additionally, it is important to feel comfortable and safe with your therapist, as the therapeutic relationship is a key factor in the success of treatment.

One of the common barriers to seeking professional help is the stigma surrounding mental health issues. Many individuals may feel embarrassed, ashamed, or afraid to reach out for help due to societal attitudes or misconceptions about mental illness. However, it is important to remember that seeking help is a sign of strength, courage, and self-awareness, not weakness or failure. Taking the step to seek professional help demonstrates a commitment to one's well-being and a desire to improve one's mental health.

Another barrier to seeking professional help is the fear of judgment or criticism from others. It is important to remember that mental health concerns are common and affect people from all walks of life. Seeking help is a wise and proactive step toward addressing and managing these concerns. Talking to a professional can provide a safe and confidential space to explore and work through your challenges without fear of judgment.

In addition to therapy and counseling, medication management can also be a helpful treatment option for certain mental health conditions, such as depression or anxiety. Medication, when prescribed and monitored by a qualified healthcare provider, can help alleviate symptoms and improve overall functioning. It is important to work closely with your healthcare provider to find the right medication and dosage that works best for you. Therapy, counseling, medication management, and other forms of treatment can provide support, guidance, and relief from mental health concerns. Remember that seeking help is a sign of strength, courage, and self-awareness, and that you deserve to live a healthy and fulfilling life. If you are struggling with mental health issues, do not hesitate to reach out for help. You are not alone, and there are professionals who are ready and willing to support you on your journey to healing and recovery.

- Taking Care of Yourself as a Parent

As a parent, it can sometimes feel like you are constantly putting the needs of your children before your own. It can be easy to neglect self-care in all its forms when you are juggling the responsibilities of parenting, work, and everyday life. However, taking care of yourself is essential not only for your own well-being but also for the well-being of your children. By prioritizing self-care, you can be a better parent, partner, and individual overall.

One important aspect of self-care as a parent is taking care of your physical health. This includes getting regular exercise, eating a balanced diet, and getting enough sleep. It can be challenging to find time for exercise and healthy eating when you have a busy schedule, but making these things a priority can have a major impact on your overall well-being. Regular exercise can help reduce stress, boost your mood, and increase your energy levels, all of which can help you be a more present and engaged parent. Eating a balanced diet can also improve your energy levels and mood, as well as help you maintain a healthy weight.

In addition to physical health, it is also important to prioritize your mental and emotional well-being as a parent. Parenting can be stressful and overwhelming at times, and it is normal to experience feelings of anxiety, frustration, and burnout. Taking care of your mental health is just as important as taking care of your physical health. This can involve finding healthy ways to cope with stress, such as practicing mindfulness or meditation, talking to a therapist or counselor, or engaging in activities that bring you joy and relaxation.

Another important aspect of self-care as a parent is setting boundaries and finding time for yourself. It can be easy to put your own needs and desires on the back burner when you are focused on taking care of your children, but it is important to remember that you are also a person with your own needs and interests. Setting boundaries with your children, partner, and others in your life can help ensure that you have the time and space to take care of yourself. This can involve saying no to activities or commitments that do not align with your priorities, delegating tasks to others when possible, and carving out time in your schedule for activities that you enjoy.

Taking care of yourself as a parent also means seeking support when you need it. Parenting can be a challenging and isolating experience, and it is important to have a support network of friends, family, and professionals who can provide guidance, advice, and emotional support. This can involve joining a parenting group or class, seeking out a mentor or coach, or talking to a therapist or counselor to help navigate the ups and downs of parenthood. Remember that asking for help is a sign of strength, not weakness, and that no parent can do it all on their own. By prioritizing self-care, you can be a happier, healthier, and more present parent. Remember to take care of your physical, mental, and emotional health, set boundaries and find time for yourself, and seek support when you need it. Parenting is a challenging but rewarding journey, and by taking care of yourself, you can be the best parent you can be.

Chapter 10: Teaching Values and Morals

- INSTILLING GOOD HABITS

Instilling good habits is an essential component of personal development and success in all areas of life. Habits are routines or behaviors that we perform regularly without much thought, and they can have a profound impact on our overall well-being and productivity. By consciously cultivating positive habits, we can improve our health, relationships, and professional performance.

One of the key aspects of instilling good habits is understanding the role of consistency and repetition. In order for a habit to become ingrained, it must be practiced consistently over time. This means committing to a behavior on a daily or regular basis and making it a priority in your routine. By repeatedly performing a certain action, it becomes easier and more automatic over time, eventually becoming second nature. This is why it is important to start small and gradually build up the habit, rather than trying to make drastic changes all at once.

Another important factor in developing good habits is setting clear goals and intentions. Before embarking on a new habit, it is crucial to identify why you want to adopt this behavior and what specific outcomes you hope to achieve. By having a clear sense of purpose and direction, you are more likely to stay motivated and committed to the habit, even when faced with challenges or setbacks. It can also be helpful to track your progress and celebrate your successes along the way, as this can reinforce positive behavior and encourage you to continue.

In addition to consistency and goal-setting, creating a supportive environment is also key to instilling good habits. Surrounding yourself with people who share similar values and goals can provide motivation and accountability, making it easier to stay on track with your habits. It can also be helpful to remove obstacles or distractions that may hinder your progress, such as unhealthy food in your pantry or excessive screen time. By making your environment conducive to your desired habits, you are setting yourself up for success and making it easier to maintain your new behaviors in the long run.

Furthermore, it is important to recognize that developing good habits is a gradual process that requires patience and perseverance. It is natural to experience setbacks or slip-ups along the way, but it is important not to get discouraged and give up. Instead, view these challenges as opportunities for growth and learning, and use them as motivation to recommit to your habits. Remember that building good habits is a journey, not a destination, and that it is okay to make mistakes as long as you are willing to learn from them and keep moving forward. By cultivating positive behaviors through consistency, goal-setting, a supportive environment, and perseverance, you can create lasting change in your life and achieve your desired outcomes. Whether you are looking to improve your health, boost your productivity, or enhance your relationships, developing good habits can help you reach your full potential and live a more fulfilling and balanced life. Start small, stay committed, and be patient with yourself – the rewards of instilling good habits are well worth the effort.

- Teaching Empathy and Compassion

Empathy and compassion are essential qualities that play a significant role in our daily interactions and relationships with others. These qualities allow us to understand and resonate with the experiences and emotions of those around us, leading to greater understanding and connection. Teaching empathy and compassion is crucial in fostering a nurturing and supportive environment where individuals feel understood, valued, and cared for.

One of the key ways in which empathy and compassion can be taught is through modeling. As educators, parents, and mentors, we serve as role models for the younger generation, demonstrating through our actions and words how to empathize and show compassion towards others. By embodying these qualities ourselves, we set an example for others to follow and create a culture of empathy and compassion within our communities.

Another important aspect of teaching empathy and compassion is through active listening and perspective-taking. Encouraging individuals to listen attentively to others, to seek to understand their perspectives, and to empathize with their emotions helps cultivate a sense of connection and understanding. By engaging in active listening and perspective-taking, individuals can develop a deeper understanding of others' experiences and emotions, leading to increased empathy and compassion.

In addition to modeling and active listening, teaching empathy and compassion can also be done through storytelling and narratives. Sharing stories that highlight acts of empathy and compassion, as well as the impact of these qualities on individuals and communities, can inspire others to cultivate these qualities within themselves. By exposing individuals to diverse narratives that showcase the power of empathy and compassion, we can help instill a sense of empathy and compassion within them.

Furthermore, incorporating empathy and compassion into the curriculum and educational programs can also play a crucial role in teaching these qualities. By integrating lessons and activities that focus on empathy, compassion, and emotional intelligence, educators can provide students with the necessary skills and knowledge to cultivate these qualities within themselves. Through interactive and experiential learning opportunities, students can practice and develop their empathy and compassion skills in a supportive and nurturing environment.

Moreover, promoting empathy and compassion in schools and educational settings can also help create a more inclusive and supportive learning environment. By fostering a culture of empathy and compassion, educators can create a sense of belonging and connection among students, leading to improved academic performance, mental well-being, and social relationships. Creating a safe and supportive space where empathy and compassion are valued can have a positive impact on the overall school climate and student success. By modeling these qualities, encouraging active listening and perspective-taking, sharing stories and narratives, integrating empathy and compassion into educational programs, and creating a supportive learning environment, we can help individuals develop a deeper sense of empathy and compassion towards others. Through these efforts, we can cultivate a culture of empathy and compassion that promotes understanding, connection, and positive relationships within our communities.

- Addressing Morally Challenging Situations

Addressing morally challenging situations is a complex and multifaceted task that requires thoughtful consideration and decision-making. In today's society, individuals are often faced with difficult choices that can have significant ethical implications. These situations may arise in various contexts, such as the workplace, relationships, or personal beliefs, and can test one's values and principles.

One common morally challenging situation that individuals may encounter is deciding whether to speak up in the face of wrongdoing or remain silent. This dilemma can be particularly difficult when there are potential consequences for speaking out, such as retaliation or damage to one's reputation. In these cases, individuals must weigh the moral imperative to do what is right against the potential risks involved. It is important for individuals to consider the greater good and the impact of their actions on others when faced with such ethical dilemmas.

Another morally challenging situation that individuals may face is choosing between competing values or principles. For example, a person may have to decide between telling the truth and protecting a friend's feelings, or between upholding their beliefs and compromising for the sake of harmony. These situations can be emotionally taxing and can force individuals to confront their own values and priorities. In these cases, it is important for individuals to reflect on their beliefs and consider the consequences of their actions before making a decision.

Addressing morally challenging situations also requires individuals to consider the perspectives of others and to practice empathy and understanding. It is essential to recognize that different people may have different values and beliefs, and that what may be morally acceptable to one person may not be to another. By engaging in open and respectful dialogue, individuals can learn from one another and work towards finding a solution that aligns with their shared values and principles. By considering the consequences of their actions, reflecting on their values and beliefs, and practicing empathy and understanding, individuals can make informed decisions that uphold their moral principles and promote ethical behavior. It is important for individuals to remember that no situation is entirely black and white, and that moral ambiguity is a natural part of life. By approaching morally challenging situations with an open mind and a willingness to engage in difficult conversations, individuals can navigate these dilemmas with grace and integrity.

Chapter 11: Balancing Work and Parenting

- TIME MANAGEMENT TIPS

Time management is a crucial skill that everyone should strive to master in order to achieve success in both their personal and professional lives. Effectively managing your time can lead to increased productivity, reduced stress, and a better work-life balance. In this article, we will discuss some key time management tips that can help you make the most of your precious hours.

One of the most important time management tips is to prioritize your tasks. This involves identifying the most important and urgent tasks on your to-do list and focusing on them first. By prioritizing your tasks, you can ensure that you are spending your time on the most crucial activities that will have the biggest impact on your goals. One helpful strategy is to use a prioritization matrix, such as the Eisenhower Matrix, to rank tasks based on their importance and urgency. This can help you identify which tasks to tackle first and which can wait until later.

Another key time management tip is to set specific goals and deadlines for each task. By breaking down your larger goals into smaller, actionable steps and setting deadlines for each step, you can create a roadmap for achieving your objectives. This can help you stay focused and motivated, as you will have a clear plan of action to guide your efforts. Additionally, setting deadlines can help prevent procrastination and ensure that you are making progress towards your goals on a consistent basis.

In addition to setting goals and deadlines, it is important to create a daily or weekly schedule to help you manage your time effectively. A schedule can help you allocate time for each task, minimize distractions, and ensure that you are making progress on your most important priorities. When creating your schedule, be sure to block out time for high-priority tasks, as well as time for breaks and relaxation. This can help you maintain a healthy work-life balance and prevent burnout.

Another valuable time management tip is to eliminate time-wasting activities and distractions. In today's digital age, it is easy to get caught up in checking emails, scrolling through social media, or engaging in other non-essential activities that eat away at your time. To combat this, try to limit your time on social media, set specific times for checking emails, and use tools such as website blockers to prevent distractions. By eliminating these time-wasters, you can free up more time for important tasks and activities.

Furthermore, it is important to learn to delegate tasks and say no when necessary. Many people struggle with trying to do everything themselves, which can lead to overwhelm and burnout. By delegating tasks to others who are capable of completing them, you can free up your time to focus on more strategic or high-value activities. Similarly, learning to say no to requests that are not in line with your priorities can help you protect your time and energy for tasks that truly matter.

Lastly, it is important to regularly evaluate and adjust your time management strategies. What works for one person may not work for another, so it is important to experiment with different techniques and find what works best for you. Periodically review your goals, schedule, and tasks to ensure that you are on track to achieve your objectives. Make adjustments as needed to optimize your time management practices and improve your overall efficiency and effectiveness. By prioritizing tasks, setting goals and deadlines, creating a schedule, eliminating distractions, delegating tasks, and regularly evaluating your strategies, you can make the most of your time and accomplish your goals with greater ease. Implementing these time management tips can help you boost your productivity, reduce stress, and achieve a better work-life balance. Remember that time is a finite resource, so it is important to use it wisely and make the most of every moment.

- Setting Priorities

Setting priorities is a crucial aspect of managing our time and resources effectively. It involves identifying what tasks, goals, or projects are most important and focusing our attention and energy on them. Prioritizing helps us make the most of our limited time and resources, ensuring that we are working towards what truly matters to us. In this essay, we will delve deeper into the concept of setting priorities, explore the benefits of doing so, and provide practical tips on how to prioritize effectively.

One of the key benefits of setting priorities is that it helps us stay focused and organized. By clearly defining what is most important to us, we can allocate our time and resources in a way that aligns with our goals and values. When we have a clear set of priorities, we are less likely to be overwhelmed by a multitude of tasks and commitments, as we can concentrate on what truly matters. This focus and clarity enable us to work more efficiently and productively, leading to better outcomes and a greater sense of accomplishment.

Setting priorities also allows us to make informed decisions about how to spend our time and energy. When we have a clear understanding of what is most important to us, we can make conscious choices about where to invest our resources. This means that we can say no to tasks or activities that do not align with our priorities, freeing up more time and energy for the things that truly matter. Prioritizing helps us avoid the trap of busyness for the sake of busyness and enables us to make deliberate choices that support our long-term goals and values.

Furthermore, setting priorities can enhance our overall sense of well-being and fulfillment. When we focus on what is truly important to us, we are more likely to feel a sense of purpose and meaning in our lives. This can increase our motivation and drive, leading to greater levels of satisfaction and happiness. By prioritizing what matters most, we are able to create a sense of balance and harmony in our lives, as we are spending our time and energy on what brings us joy and fulfillment. In this way, setting priorities can lead to a more fulfilling and meaningful existence.

To prioritize effectively, it is important to first identify what is most important to us. This involves reflecting on our goals, values, and priorities in different areas of our lives, such as work, relationships, health, and personal development. By clarifying what matters most to us, we can create a hierarchy of priorities that guides our decision-making and actions. It is also helpful to consider the urgency and importance of different tasks and goals, as this can help us determine where to focus our attention and resources.

Once we have identified our priorities, it is essential to create a plan of action. This involves breaking down our goals and tasks into smaller, manageable steps and scheduling them into our daily or weekly routine. By creating a roadmap for how to achieve our priorities, we can ensure that we are making progress towards our goals and staying on track. It is also important to regularly review and reassess our priorities, as our circumstances and goals may change over time. By identifying what is most important to us and focusing our attention and energy on those priorities, we can increase our focus, productivity, and sense of fulfillment. Prioritizing enables us to make informed decisions about how to spend our time and resources, leading to better outcomes and a greater sense of well-being. By following the practical tips outlined in this essay, we can prioritize effectively and achieve our goals with clarity and purpose.

- Maintaining a Healthy Work-life Balance

Maintaining a healthy work-life balance is essential for overall well-being and productivity. As individuals strive to succeed in their careers and achieve personal goals, it is important to remember that excessive work can lead to burnout and negatively impact mental and physical health. In today's fast-paced world, where technology allows for constant connectivity and accessibility, it is crucial to establish boundaries between work and personal life to prevent work from taking over and causing stress and exhaustion.

One key aspect of maintaining a healthy work-life balance is setting clear boundaries between work and personal time. This can include establishing specific work hours and sticking to them, avoiding checking work emails or messages outside of those hours, and prioritizing personal commitments and activities. By clearly defining when work begins and ends, individuals can create a sense of separation and allow themselves to fully engage in their personal lives without the constant intrusion of work-related tasks.

Another important factor in maintaining a healthy work-life balance is prioritizing self-care and well-being. This can involve engaging in activities that promote relaxation and stress reduction, such as exercise, meditation, or hobbies. Taking time to unwind and recharge is critical for overall mental and physical health, and can help individuals feel more energized and focused when they return to work. Additionally, ensuring proper nutrition, adequate sleep, and regular physical activity are essential components of a healthy lifestyle that can help individuals effectively manage the demands of work and personal life.

Effective time management is also crucial for maintaining a healthy work-life balance. By prioritizing tasks, setting realistic goals, and utilizing tools such as to-do lists and calendars, individuals can better manage their workload and allocate time for both work and personal activities. It is important to recognize that it is not always possible to complete every task or meet every deadline, and that it is okay to ask for help or delegate responsibilities when needed. By effectively managing time and tasks, individuals can reduce stress and prevent feeling overwhelmed by work obligations.

Communication is another key element in maintaining a healthy work-life balance. It is important for individuals to communicate their needs and boundaries to employers, colleagues, and family members to ensure they are able to effectively balance their work and personal commitments. This can involve setting expectations with employers about work hours and availability, as well as clearly communicating personal responsibilities and commitments to family members. By fostering open and honest communication, individuals can reduce misunderstandings and conflicts that can arise from blurred boundaries between work and personal life. By setting clear boundaries, prioritizing self-care, managing time effectively, and communicating openly, individuals can find a harmonious balance between their work and personal lives. It is important to remember that it is okay to prioritize personal well-being and happiness, and to make choices that support a healthy and fulfilling lifestyle. By incorporating these strategies into daily routines, individuals can achieve a sense of balance and fulfillment that enhances both their professional and personal lives.

Chapter 12: Navigating Technology and Social Media

- SETTING SCREEN TIME Limits

Screen time limits have become increasingly important in today's digital age as more and more people of all ages are spending a considerable amount of time in front of screens. Whether it's computers, smartphones, tablets, or televisions, the amount of time spent on these devices can have a significant impact on our physical and mental health. Setting screen time limits is a proactive approach to managing the amount of time spent on screens and can help individuals lead a more balanced and healthy lifestyle.

One of the most important reasons to set screen time limits is to prevent the negative effects that excessive screen time can have on our health. Studies have shown that prolonged screen time can lead to a variety of health issues, including obesity, poor sleep quality, eye strain, and even mental health problems.

Setting screen time limits can also help individuals increase their productivity and focus on other important aspects of their lives. When we spend too much time on screens, we often neglect other activities that are essential for our physical and mental health, such as exercise, socializing with friends and family, and engaging in hobbies. By setting limits on screen time, individuals can make more time for these activities and ultimately lead a more fulfilling and balanced life.

It is important to note that setting screen time limits does not mean completely banning screens from our lives. Screens play a crucial role in our daily lives, and it is unrealistic to completely eliminate them. Instead, setting reasonable limits on screen time can help individuals strike a healthy balance between using screens for work, entertainment, and communication, while also making time for other important activities.

When setting screen time limits, it is important to consider the individual needs and circumstances of each person. For example, children and teenagers may require different screen time limits than adults, as their developmental needs and cognitive abilities are different. Additionally, individuals who rely on screens for work or education may need to set different limits than those who use screens primarily for entertainment.

There are several strategies that individuals can use to set effective screen time limits. One approach is to set specific time limits for different activities, such as allowing a certain amount of time for social media, gaming, or watching TV. Another approach is to set designated screen-free times, such as during meals, before bedtime, or during family activities. By implementing these strategies, individuals can gradually reduce their screen time and develop healthier screen habits.

In addition to setting screen time limits, it is important to also monitor and track screen time usage to ensure that limits are being followed. There are several apps and tools available that can help individuals track their screen time and set reminders to take breaks or limit usage. By staying accountable and aware of their screen time habits, individuals can make more informed choices about how they spend their time on screens. By finding a balance between using screens for work, entertainment, and communication, and making time for other important activities, individuals can lead a more fulfilling and balanced life in today's digital age.

- Teaching Online Safety

Teaching online safety is an essential skill that all individuals should possess in today's digital age. With the increasing reliance on technology for communication, information, and entertainment, it is crucial to be aware of the potential threats that exist online and how to protect ourselves from them. Online safety encompasses a range of topics, including protecting personal information, recognizing scams and phishing attempts, and understanding the risks associated with social media and online interactions. By educating individuals on these topics, we can help them navigate the online world safely and confidently.

One of the first steps in teaching online safety is to emphasize the importance of protecting personal information. This includes not sharing sensitive information, such as passwords, social security numbers, and financial information, with unknown or untrusted sources. Individuals should also be cautious about what they share on social media platforms, as this information can be easily accessed by malicious parties. Encouraging individuals to use strong, unique passwords for each online account and enabling two-factor authentication can also help protect sensitive information from being compromised.

Another important aspect of online safety is being able to recognize scams and phishing attempts. Scams are fraudulent schemes designed to deceive individuals into providing personal information or money to the scammer. Phishing is a type of scam that involves sending fake emails or messages that appear to be from legitimate sources, such as banks or government agencies, in order to trick individuals into revealing sensitive information. By teaching individuals how to identify these types of scams and phishing attempts, we can help them avoid falling victim to these deceitful tactics.

Social media and online interactions present their own set of risks when it comes to online safety. Individuals should be mindful of the information they share on social media platforms, as this information can be used by cybercriminals to target them. Additionally, individuals should be cautious about interacting with strangers online and should never meet up with someone they have only met online without first verifying their identity and intentions. By teaching individuals about the potential risks associated with social media and online interactions, we can help them make informed decisions about how they engage with others online.

In addition to educating individuals on these specific aspects of online safety, it is important to foster a culture of digital literacy and critical thinking. This includes teaching individuals how to evaluate the credibility of online sources, how to fact-check information, and how to spot misinformation and fake news. By promoting critical thinking skills, we can help individuals navigate the vast amount of information available online and make informed decisions about what to believe and share. By educating individuals on how to protect their personal information, recognize scams and phishing attempts, understand the risks of social media and online interactions, and develop digital literacy skills, we can empower them to navigate the online world safely and confidently. With the right tools and knowledge, individuals can harness the power of technology while staying safe and secure online.

- Monitoring Your Child's Online Activity

Monitoring your child's online activity is an important aspect of parenting in today's digital age. With the prevalence of smartphones, tablets, and computers, children have access to a world of information and communication at their fingertips. While the internet can be a valuable tool for learning and entertainment, it can also pose risks to children's safety and well-being. By monitoring your child's online activity, you can help protect them from potential dangers and provide guidance on how to use the internet responsibly.

One of the key reasons to monitor your child's online activity is to protect them from exposure to inappropriate content. The internet is full of websites, videos, and images that may not be suitable for children. By keeping an eye on the websites your child visits and the content they interact with, you can ensure that they are not exposed to harmful or age-inappropriate material. This can help protect their mental and emotional well-being and prevent them from being exposed to content that may be disturbing or damaging.

In addition to protecting your child from inappropriate content, monitoring their online activity can also help you keep them safe from online predators and cyberbullying. The internet provides a platform for individuals to communicate and interact with others, which can be both positive and negative. Unfortunately, there are individuals who may seek to harm or exploit children online. By monitoring your child's communications and social media activity, you can be on the lookout for any signs of predatory behavior or cyberbullying. This can allow you to intervene early and protect your child from potential harm.

Another important reason to monitor your child's online activity is to help them develop healthy digital habits. The internet can be a source of endless distraction and entertainment, which can sometimes lead to excessive screen time and neglect of other important activities. By setting limits on your child's internet usage and monitoring the websites and apps they use, you can help them develop a balanced approach to technology. Encouraging your child to engage in offline activities such as exercise, hobbies, and socializing can help them maintain a healthy balance between their online and offline lives.

Monitoring your child's online activity can also provide an opportunity for open communication and education about internet safety. By discussing the risks and benefits of the internet with your child, you can help them understand the importance of being cautious and responsible online. Talking to your child about the potential dangers of sharing personal information, interacting with strangers, and engaging in risky behaviors online can empower them to make informed decisions and protect themselves. By maintaining an open dialogue about online safety, you can create a supportive and trusting relationship with your child that encourages them to come to you with any concerns or questions. By staying informed about your child's online behaviors and interactions, you can help protect them from potential dangers, teach them healthy digital habits, and empower them to make safe choices online. By engaging with your child in conversations about internet safety and setting clear boundaries and expectations, you can create a safe and supportive environment that promotes responsible internet use. Remember that monitoring your child's online activity is not about invading their privacy, but rather about guiding and supporting them in navigating the digital world with confidence and awareness.

Chapter 13: Developing a Positive Parenting Style

- AUTHORITATIVE VS. Authoritarian Parenting

Parenting styles play a crucial role in shaping a child's behavior, personality, and overall development. Two common parenting styles that are often confused but have significant differences are authoritative and authoritarian parenting. These two styles have distinct approaches to discipline, communication, and expectations, which can have a profound impact on a child's well-being.

Authoritative parenting is characterized by providing structure and guidance while also being responsive and nurturing towards the child's needs. Parents who follow this style set clear rules and boundaries but also encourage open communication and independence. They strive to explain the reasoning behind their rules and decisions, fostering a sense of understanding and trust between themselves and their child. Authoritative parents also show warmth and empathy towards their children, creating a supportive and loving environment for them to thrive in.

On the other hand, authoritarian parenting is characterized by strict rules and high demands with little room for flexibility or negotiation. Parents who follow this style tend to have high expectations for their children's behavior and performance, often enforcing obedience through punishment or threats. Communication in authoritarian parenting is typically one-way, with little opportunity for the child to express their thoughts or feelings. This approach can lead to a lack of trust and emotional connection between the parent and child, as well as feelings of resentment and rebellion in the child.

It is essential to understand the impact of these parenting styles on a child's development. Research has shown that authoritative parenting is associated with positive outcomes, such as higher self-esteem, better academic performance, and improved social skills. Children raised in an authoritative environment are more likely to develop independence, problem-solving skills, and emotional intelligence. They are also less likely to engage in risky behaviors or exhibit aggressive tendencies.

In contrast, authoritarian parenting has been linked to negative outcomes in children, including lower self-esteem, poorer academic performance, and difficulties in forming healthy relationships. Children raised in an authoritarian environment may struggle to develop confidence, independence, and problem-solving skills. They may also be more prone to anxiety, depression, and behavioral issues due to the lack of emotional support and autonomy in their upbringing.

One key difference between authoritative and authoritarian parenting is the underlying philosophy and approach to discipline. Authoritative parents believe in using positive reinforcement and logical consequences to teach their children right from wrong. They aim to guide and support their child's behavior, helping them learn to make their own choices and understand the consequences of their actions. In contrast, authoritarian parents tend to rely on punishment and strict discipline as a means of control. They may use fear, threats, and harsh consequences to enforce compliance and obedience in their child.

Another crucial distinction between these parenting styles is the communication dynamics between parent and child. Authoritative parents prioritize open, honest, and respectful communication with their children. They encourage dialogue, active listening, and empathy, creating a safe space for their child to express their thoughts and feelings. This approach fosters trust, connection, and mutual understanding between parent and child. In contrast, authoritarian parents often use a top-down communication style, where directives are given without explanation or consideration for the child's perspective. This can lead to misunderstandings, conflicts, and a breakdown in the parent-child relationship.

It is important for parents to be aware of their parenting style and its implications on their child's well-being. While it is natural for parents to have different strengths, weaknesses, and approaches to parenting, understanding the differences between authoritative and authoritarian styles can help them make informed decisions about how they interact with their child. By striving to be more authoritative in their parenting approach, parents can create a supportive, nurturing, and empowering environment for their child to grow and thrive. This not only benefits the child's development but also strengthens the bond between parent and child for years to come.

- Permissive vs. Neglectful Parenting

Parenting styles play a crucial role in shaping the development and behavior of children. Two contrasting styles that have been widely studied and discussed in the field of psychology are permissive and neglectful parenting. While both styles involve low levels of control and demands placed on children, they differ in their levels of warmth and responsiveness. Permissive parents tend to be indulgent and lenient, while neglectful parents are indifferent and uninvolved in their children's lives.

Permissive parenting is characterized by high levels of warmth and low levels of control. These parents are responsive to their children's needs and desires, often giving in to their demands and providing few rules or boundaries. Permissive parents tend to prioritize their children's happiness and comfort over discipline and structure, resulting in children who may struggle with self-regulation and impulse control. While permissive parenting can create a nurturing and supportive environment for children, it can also lead to difficulties in setting limits and boundaries, which are essential for healthy development.

On the other hand, neglectful parenting is characterized by low levels of warmth and control. These parents are often disengaged and uninvolved in their children's lives, failing to provide the emotional support and guidance that children need to thrive. Neglectful parents may be preoccupied with their own concerns and neglect their children's basic needs, leading to feelings of abandonment and insecurity in their children. As a result, children raised in neglectful environments may struggle with emotional regulation, have lower self-esteem, and experience difficulties in forming healthy relationships.

It is important to note that both permissive and neglectful parenting styles can have negative consequences for children's development. While permissive parents may foster a sense of independence and autonomy in their children, they may also struggle with setting boundaries and limits, leading to behavioral problems and difficulties in academic and social settings. Neglectful parents, on the other hand, may fail to provide the emotional support and guidance that children need to thrive, resulting in feelings of insecurity and low self-worth.

In order to promote healthy development and well-being in children, it is important for parents to strive for a balance between warmth and control in their parenting approach. Authoritative parenting, which combines high levels of warmth and responsiveness with clear and consistent rules and boundaries, has been found to be the most effective parenting style in promoting positive outcomes for children. Authoritative parents provide emotional support and guidance while also setting expectations and consequences for behavior, helping children develop essential skills such as self-control, resilience, and empathy. While permissive parents may prioritize their children's happiness and comfort over discipline and structure, neglectful parents may be disengaged and uninvolved in their children's lives. Both styles can have negative consequences for children's development, highlighting the importance of finding a balance between warmth and control in parenting. Authoritative parenting, which combines high levels of warmth and responsiveness with clear expectations and consequences, has been found to be the most effective approach in promoting positive outcomes for children. By fostering a supportive and structured environment, parents can help their children develop essential skills for success and well-being.

- Finding Your Own Parenting Style

Parenting style refers to the approach and strategies that parents use to raise their children. It is shaped by a combination of cultural beliefs, personal experiences, and individual personality traits. Finding your own parenting style is a process that involves self-reflection, trial and error, and continuous learning. There is no one-size-fits-all approach to parenting, as every child is unique and will respond differently to various parenting styles.

One of the first steps in finding your own parenting style is to reflect on your own upbringing and how it has shaped your beliefs and attitudes towards parenting. This may involve thinking about the ways in which your own parents raised you, both positive and negative, and considering how these experiences have influenced your own parenting choices. It can be helpful to identify what aspects of your own upbringing you would like to emulate and what aspects you may want to do differently. This self-reflection can help you gain insight into your own parenting values and priorities.

Another important step in finding your own parenting style is to consider your child's individual needs, temperament, and developmental stage. Children have unique personalities and may require different approaches to discipline, communication, and guidance. It is important to be flexible and adaptable in your parenting approach, taking into account your child's personality and needs. This may involve adjusting your parenting style as your child grows and develops, and being willing to try different strategies to see what works best for your child.

As you navigate the process of finding your own parenting style, it is important to seek out resources and support from other parents, professionals, and experts in child development. This may include attending parenting workshops, reading parenting books, and seeking advice from trusted friends and family members. It can be helpful to stay informed about the latest research and trends in parenting, while also trusting your own instincts and intuition as a parent. Remember that there is no one "right" way to parent, and that it is okay to make mistakes and learn from them along the way.

Ultimately, finding your own parenting style is a journey of self-discovery and growth. It requires a willingness to reflect on your own values and beliefs, adapt to your child's individual needs, and seek out support and resources as needed. By approaching parenting with an open mind and a willingness to learn, you can develop a parenting style that is unique to you and your child, and that fosters a loving and supportive relationship. Remember that parenting is a marathon, not a sprint, and that it is okay to evolve and change as you learn and grow along the way.

Chapter 14: Promoting Academic Success

- CREATING A POSITIVE Learning Environment

Creating a positive learning environment is crucial in ensuring that students can thrive and reach their full potential. A positive learning environment is one where students feel safe, supported, and encouraged to take risks and make mistakes. This type of environment fosters a sense of belonging and community, which can have a profound impact on students' academic success and overall well-being.

One key aspect of creating a positive learning environment is the physical space itself. The physical environment of a classroom can greatly influence students' attitudes and behaviors towards learning. A well-organized and visually appealing classroom can help create a sense of calm and order, while also inspiring creativity and curiosity. It is important to create a space that is conducive to learning, with plenty of natural light, comfortable seating, and resources readily available for students to use.

In addition to the physical environment, the emotional and social climate of the classroom also plays a significant role in creating a positive learning environment. Teachers can cultivate a positive classroom culture by promoting a sense of respect, empathy, and cooperation among students. This can be achieved through various strategies, such as establishing clear expectations for behavior, actively promoting positive peer relationships, and addressing conflicts and issues in a constructive manner.

Furthermore, teachers can create a positive learning environment by fostering a growth mindset among students. A growth mindset is the belief that intelligence and abilities can be developed through effort and perseverance. By encouraging students to see challenges as opportunities for growth and learning, teachers can help build students' confidence and resilience in the face of setbacks. This can lead to improvements in students' motivation, engagement, and academic performance.

Another important aspect of creating a positive learning environment is providing students with opportunities for autonomy and choice in their learning. When students feel that they have some control over their learning process, they are more likely to be motivated and engaged in their work. Teachers can promote autonomy by providing students with options for how they demonstrate their understanding of concepts, allowing them to work at their own pace, and giving them opportunities to pursue their own interests and passions.

In summary, creating a positive learning environment involves a combination of physical, emotional, and cognitive elements that work together to support students' academic and social development. By establishing a welcoming and supportive atmosphere, promoting a growth mindset, and providing opportunities for autonomy and choice, teachers can help create an environment where students feel inspired, empowered, and motivated to learn and grow. Ultimately, a positive learning environment is essential for fostering students' success and well-being in the classroom and beyond.

- Supporting Homework and Study Habits

Supporting homework and study habits is crucial for academic success and overall well-being. Developing effective study habits and a consistent homework routine is essential for students to retain information, master concepts, and succeed in their academic pursuits. As educators and parents, it is our responsibility to provide students with the necessary tools and support to help them develop these important skills.

One of the key factors in supporting homework and study habits is creating a designated study space. This space should be quiet, free from distractions, and conducive to learning. Students should have access to all necessary materials, such as textbooks, notebooks, pens, and pencils, in order to complete their assignments efficiently. It is important to establish a routine and set aside a specific time each day for studying and completing homework. This consistency helps students develop a sense of responsibility and discipline, leading to better time management and academic performance.

In addition to creating a conducive study environment, it is also important to teach students effective study strategies. Encouraging students to take notes, highlight key concepts, and create study guides can help them retain information and better understand complex topics. Breaking up study sessions into smaller, manageable chunks can also improve retention and comprehension. Encourage students to review their notes and materials regularly, rather than cramming the night before a test. This will help them internalize the information and perform better on assessments.

Furthermore, offering support and encouragement is essential in fostering good homework and study habits. Providing positive reinforcement and praise for hard work and achievements can motivate students to continue putting in their best effort. It is important to be patient and understanding, as every student learns at their own pace. Offering assistance and guidance when needed can help students overcome challenges and build confidence in their abilities. Encourage open communication and let students know that it is okay to ask for help when they are struggling.

Another important aspect of supporting homework and study habits is encouraging balance and self-care. It is important for students to take breaks, get enough rest, and engage in activities that promote physical and mental well-being. Encourage students to participate in extracurricular activities, spend time with friends and family, and engage in hobbies they enjoy. A well-rounded lifestyle contributes to overall academic success and personal fulfillment. It is important to prioritize self-care and teach students the importance of maintaining a healthy work-life balance. By creating a conducive study environment, teaching effective study strategies, offering support and encouragement, and encouraging balance and self-care, educators and parents can help students develop the skills they need to excel academically. By fostering a positive and supportive learning environment, students will be better equipped to achieve their goals, fulfill their potential, and succeed in their academic endeavors. Let us continue to prioritize the development of good study habits and homework routines in order to set students up for success both in school and in life.

- Communicating with Teachers

Communicating with teachers is an essential aspect of a student's educational experience. Whether it be to clarify assignments, seek help understanding material, or simply to build a positive relationship with an instructor, effective communication with teachers can greatly impact a student's academic success. While the thought of approaching a teacher may seem intimidating to some, it is important to remember that teachers are there to support and guide students in their learning journey.

One key aspect of effective communication with teachers is to be proactive. This means reaching out to your teacher before issues arise, rather than waiting until a problem becomes too big to handle. If you are struggling with a concept or assignment, don't hesitate to ask for clarification or additional support. Most teachers appreciate when students take initiative and show a genuine interest in their education.

When communicating with teachers, it is important to be respectful and professional. This means using appropriate language and tone when addressing your teacher, whether that be in person, via email, or through other forms of communication. Remember that teachers are professionals who deserve to be treated with respect. Be sure to address your teacher by their preferred title and avoid using slang or informal language.

In addition to being proactive and respectful, it is important to be specific in your communication with teachers. When seeking help or clarification on an assignment, be clear about what you need assistance with. This will help your teacher understand how best to support you and provide the necessary guidance. Avoid vague or ambiguous language that could lead to misunderstandings.

Another important aspect of effective communication with teachers is to actively listen to their feedback and suggestions. Teachers are there to help you succeed, so it is important to take their advice seriously and make an effort to incorporate it into your learning process. Remember that teachers have a wealth of knowledge and experience that can be beneficial to your academic growth.

Lastly, building a positive relationship with your teachers can greatly enhance your educational experience. Show your appreciation for their hard work and dedication by expressing gratitude when they go above and beyond to help you succeed. Take the time to get to know your teachers on a personal level and show genuine interest in their classes and teachings. A positive relationship with your teachers can make the learning process more enjoyable and productive. By being proactive, respectful, specific, and receptive to feedback, students can build positive relationships with their teachers and maximize their learning potential. Remember that teachers are there to support and guide you in your educational journey, so don't hesitate to reach out to them for help and guidance. By fostering strong communication with your teachers, you can create a more enriching and rewarding educational experience.

Chapter 15: Encouraging Healthy Habits

- NUTRITION GUIDELINES

Nutrition guidelines are important recommendations that are designed to help individuals make informed and healthy choices about their diet and overall nutrition. These guidelines are developed by experts in the field of nutrition and are based on scientific research and evidence. They provide a framework for individuals to follow in order to ensure that they are meeting their nutritional needs and maintaining good health.

One of the key aspects of nutrition guidelines is the importance of a balanced diet. A balanced diet is one that includes a variety of nutrients from all the different food groups. This includes fruits, vegetables, whole grains, protein sources, and dairy products. By including a variety of foods in your diet, you can ensure that you are getting all the essential nutrients that your body needs to function properly.

In addition to a balanced diet, nutrition guidelines also emphasize the importance of portion control. Portion control is essential for maintaining a healthy weight and preventing overeating. It involves being mindful of the amount of food you are consuming and not eating more than your body needs. By practicing portion control, you can prevent weight gain and reduce your risk of developing chronic diseases such as obesity and diabetes.

Another important aspect of nutrition guidelines is the recommendation to limit the consumption of certain foods that are high in unhealthy fats, sugars, and sodium. These foods, such as fast food, processed foods, sugary beverages, and snacks, are often low in nutrients and high in calories. By limiting your intake of these foods, you can reduce your risk of developing heart disease, diabetes, and other health problems.

Nutrition guidelines also stress the importance of staying hydrated and drinking an adequate amount of water each day. Water is essential for various bodily functions, including digestion, nutrient absorption, and regulating body temperature. By staying hydrated, you can ensure that your body is functioning properly and support your overall health and well-being. By following these guidelines, you can ensure that you are meeting your nutritional needs and maintaining good health. A balanced diet, portion control, limiting unhealthy foods, and staying hydrated are all key components of nutrition guidelines that can help you achieve optimal health and well-being. By incorporating these guidelines into your daily routine, you can improve your overall health and reduce your risk of developing chronic diseases.

- Physical Activity Recommendations

Physical activity recommendations are important guidelines that provide individuals with guidance on the amount and intensity of exercise necessary to achieve optimal health and well-being. These recommendations are based on scientific research and are designed to help individuals improve their cardiovascular fitness, muscular strength, flexibility, and overall health. By following these guidelines, individuals can reduce their risk of developing chronic diseases such as heart disease, diabetes, and obesity, and improve their quality of life.

One of the key components of physical activity recommendations is the amount of exercise that individuals should aim to achieve each week. The current guidelines recommend that adults engage in at least 150 minutes of moderate-intensity aerobic exercise or 75 minutes of vigorous-intensity aerobic exercise each week. This can be broken down into smaller increments, such as 30 minutes of exercise on most days of the week. For even greater health benefits, individuals can aim for 300 minutes of moderate-intensity exercise or 150 minutes of vigorous-intensity exercise each week.

In addition to aerobic exercise, physical activity recommendations also include recommendations for strength training and flexibility exercises. Strength training is important for maintaining muscle mass and bone density, especially as individuals age. The guidelines recommend that adults engage in strength training exercises at least two days a week, targeting all major muscle groups. This can include using resistance bands, free weights, or weight machines. Flexibility exercises, such as yoga or stretching, are also important for maintaining range of motion in the joints and preventing injury. The recommendations suggest engaging in flexibility exercises at least two days a week.

It is important to note that physical activity recommendations may vary depending on an individual's age, fitness level, and health status. For example, older adults may need to engage in more flexibility exercises to maintain their range of motion, while individuals with certain health conditions may need to modify their exercise routine to ensure safety. It is always recommended to consult with a healthcare provider before starting a new exercise program, especially if you have any chronic health conditions or injuries.

Meeting the physical activity recommendations can have a significant impact on an individual's health and well-being. Regular exercise has been shown to improve cardiovascular health by reducing blood pressure, cholesterol levels, and the risk of heart disease. It can also help individuals maintain a healthy weight, reduce the risk of developing type 2 diabetes, and improve mental health by reducing symptoms of anxiety and depression. In addition, physical activity can improve sleep quality, boost energy levels, and enhance overall quality of life. By following these guidelines and engaging in regular aerobic, strength training, and flexibility exercises, individuals can improve their cardiovascular fitness, muscular strength, flexibility, and overall health. It is important to consult with a healthcare provider before starting a new exercise program, especially if you have any chronic health conditions or injuries. By incorporating physical activity into your daily routine, you can reduce your risk of developing chronic diseases, improve your quality of life, and enjoy the many benefits of a healthy and active lifestyle.

- Ensuring Adequate Sleep

Sleep is a critical component of overall health and well-being, yet many individuals struggle to get an adequate amount of quality rest each night. In today's fast-paced world, with constant demands and pressures, it can be challenging to prioritize sleep. However, research has shown that getting enough sleep is essential for cognitive function, emotional well-being, physical health, and overall productivity.

One of the key factors in ensuring adequate sleep is establishing a consistent bedtime routine. This involves creating a calming and relaxing environment in the hour or so leading up to bedtime. This may include activities such as reading a book, taking a warm bath, or practicing mindfulness or meditation. By consistently engaging in these calming activities, your body will start to recognize the cues that it is time for sleep, making it easier to fall asleep and stay asleep throughout the night.

In addition to establishing a bedtime routine, it is important to prioritize sleep hygiene. This includes creating a sleep-friendly environment by keeping your bedroom dark, cool, and quiet. It is also important to limit exposure to screens and blue light in the hours leading up to bedtime, as this type of light can disrupt your body's natural sleep-wake cycle. By making these adjustments to your sleep environment and habits, you can improve both the quality and duration of your sleep.

Another important aspect of ensuring adequate sleep is paying attention to your diet and exercise habits. Eating a balanced and nutritious diet can have a significant impact on your sleep quality. Avoiding caffeine, alcohol, and heavy meals close to bedtime can help to promote better sleep. Additionally, regular exercise can help to improve the quality of your sleep by reducing stress and promoting relaxation. However, it is important to exercise earlier in the day, as vigorous physical activity close to bedtime can actually interfere with your ability to fall asleep.

If despite your best efforts, you still struggle to get an adequate amount of sleep, it may be beneficial to seek out the advice of a healthcare professional. Chronic sleep disturbances can have a negative impact on your physical and mental health, so it is important to address any underlying issues that may be contributing to your sleep problems. A healthcare provider can help to identify potential causes of your sleep difficulties and recommend appropriate treatment options, such as cognitive-behavioral therapy for insomnia or medication if necessary. By establishing a consistent bedtime routine, prioritizing sleep hygiene, and paying attention to your diet and exercise habits, you can improve the quality and duration of your sleep. If you continue to struggle with sleep, don't hesitate to seek out the advice of a healthcare professional. With the right approach and support, you can improve your sleep and reap the numerous benefits that come with a good night's rest.

Chapter 16: Strengthening Sibling Relationships

- PROMOTING COOPERATION and Respect

Promoting cooperation and respect is essential for fostering a harmonious and productive environment in any setting, whether it be in the workplace, in school, or within a community. Cooperation involves working together effectively towards a common goal, while respect involves recognizing and valuing the opinions, beliefs, and contributions of others.

One of the key benefits of promoting cooperation and respect is the creation of a positive and inclusive culture. When individuals feel respected and valued for their unique perspectives and contributions, they are more likely to feel motivated to actively engage and participate in group activities. Furthermore, a culture of cooperation and respect can help to build strong relationships based on trust and understanding, which can ultimately lead to a more cohesive and supportive community.

In addition to fostering a positive culture, promoting cooperation and respect can also help to address and prevent conflicts within a group. By encouraging open communication, active listening, and the consideration of different viewpoints, individuals can work together to find common ground and resolve conflicts in a constructive and respectful manner. This can help to prevent misunderstandings, build trust, and enhance teamwork, ultimately leading to a more harmonious and productive environment.

Furthermore, promoting cooperation and respect can also lead to greater diversity and inclusion within a group. When individuals feel respected and valued for who they are, regardless of their background, beliefs, or identity, they are more likely to feel empowered to contribute their unique perspectives and talents. This can help to foster innovation, creativity, and a more robust decision-making process that takes into account a wide range of ideas and viewpoints. In this way, promoting cooperation and respect can help to create a more inclusive and diverse community that celebrates and values the differences among its members. By actively encouraging these values, individuals can build strong relationships, address conflicts effectively, and empower diverse perspectives and talents to thrive. By working together to promote these values, individuals can create a more harmonious and inclusive community that is built on a foundation of mutual respect, collaboration, and understanding.

- Handling Sibling Rivalry

Sibling rivalry is a common phenomenon that occurs in many families. It is the competition or animosity between siblings, often stemming from a sense of jealousy, resentment, or a desire for attention. While some degree of sibling rivalry is normal and healthy, it can become problematic when it escalates to the point of causing distress or conflict within the family. Parents and caregivers play a crucial role in managing and addressing sibling rivalry in order to foster healthy relationships between siblings.

One of the key factors in handling sibling rivalry is to understand the underlying causes. Siblings may compete for their parents' attention, affection, or resources such as toys, clothes, or privileges. This competition can be exacerbated by factors such as differences in temperament, age, gender, or birth order. Siblings may also feel threatened by each other's achievements, talents, or relationships outside the family. By identifying these triggers, parents can better anticipate and address potential sources of conflict between siblings.

Communication is essential in managing sibling rivalry. Parents can help siblings express their feelings and concerns in a constructive manner, while also setting clear boundaries and expectations for their behavior. Encouraging siblings to talk openly and honestly about their emotions can help them develop empathy, assertiveness, and conflict resolution skills. Parents can also facilitate positive interactions between siblings by encouraging them to work together on shared interests, projects, or activities. By fostering a sense of cooperation and collaboration, parents can help siblings build stronger bonds and reduce feelings of rivalry.

It is important for parents to avoid playing favorites or comparing siblings, as this can fuel feelings of jealousy and resentment. Instead, parents should acknowledge and celebrate each child's unique strengths, talents, and accomplishments. By showing equal attention and appreciation to all of their children, parents can help prevent feelings of inadequacy or competitiveness between siblings. Creating a positive and inclusive family environment where each child feels valued and respected can help reduce sibling rivalry and promote a sense of unity and harmony within the family.

Establishing and enforcing clear rules and consequences can help prevent and manage conflicts between siblings. Parents should establish consistent expectations for behavior, boundaries, and responsibilities within the family. By setting clear guidelines and holding siblings accountable for their actions, parents can help create a sense of fairness and order in the household. It is important for parents to address conflicts between siblings promptly and impartially, while also teaching them how to resolve disagreements and find mutually agreeable solutions. By modeling effective conflict resolution skills and promoting cooperation, parents can help siblings learn how to communicate and problem-solve in a respectful and constructive manner.

In some cases, sibling rivalry may be a symptom of deeper underlying issues such as low self-esteem, insecurity, or unresolved conflicts within the family. Parents should be mindful of any signs of distress or emotional turmoil in their children and seek professional help if needed. Family therapy or counseling can provide a safe and supportive environment for siblings to address their feelings, work through their differences, and strengthen their relationship. By addressing the root causes of sibling rivalry and promoting open communication and understanding, parents can help their children develop healthier and more harmonious relationships with each other. By understanding the causes of sibling rivalry, promoting positive interactions, setting clear boundaries, and seeking professional help when needed, parents can help siblings build strong and healthy relationships. Ultimately, fostering a sense of mutual respect, support, and cooperation between siblings can create a more loving and harmonious family environment for everyone involved.

- Fostering Bonding Moments

Fostering bonding moments is a crucial aspect of building strong relationships, whether it be in the workplace, within families, or among friends. These moments are not just important for creating a sense of connection and unity, but also for enhancing collaboration, communication, and trust among individuals. When people feel a sense of camaraderie and closeness with others, they are more likely to work together effectively, resolve conflicts peacefully, and support each other in times of need. It is therefore essential for individuals and groups to actively seek out opportunities to foster bonding moments in order to cultivate meaningful and lasting relationships.

One of the key ways to foster bonding moments is through engaging in shared activities and experiences. This can include anything from team-building exercises in the workplace to family game nights at home. By participating in activities together, individuals can bond over a common goal, challenge, or interest, which can help break down barriers and facilitate open communication. Shared experiences also create memories that can strengthen the bond between individuals and provide a foundation for future interactions. For example, a team that goes on a weekend retreat together may come back feeling more connected and motivated to work together towards common goals.

Another important aspect of fostering bonding moments is creating a supportive and inclusive environment where individuals feel comfortable expressing themselves and sharing their thoughts and feelings. This requires actively listening to others, showing empathy and understanding, and valuing each person's unique perspective. When people feel heard and respected, they are more likely to open up and form deeper connections with others. This can be especially important in the workplace, where trust and collaboration are essential for achieving success. By creating a culture of support and understanding, leaders can help foster bonding moments among team members and promote a positive and productive work environment.

Building trust is also a critical component of fostering bonding moments. Trust is the foundation of any strong relationship, and without it, individuals may feel hesitant to engage in meaningful conversations or share personal information with others. Trust is built through consistent and reliable behavior, open communication, and mutual respect. When people feel that they can trust others to support and respect them, they are more likely to engage in bonding moments that can create lasting connections. Building trust takes time and effort, but the benefits of a trusting relationship are well worth the investment.

In addition to fostering bonding moments through shared activities, creating a supportive environment, and building trust, it is also important to recognize the role of communication in strengthening relationships. Effective communication is key to building connections, resolving conflicts, and fostering mutual understanding among individuals. By being open and honest in your communication, listening actively to others, and being willing to compromise and find common ground, you can create a strong foundation for bonding moments to occur. Communicating clearly and effectively can help individuals express their thoughts and feelings, address misunderstandings, and build trust and respect with others.

Ultimately, fostering bonding moments is an essential aspect of building strong and meaningful relationships. By engaging in shared activities, creating a supportive environment, building trust, and communicating effectively, individuals and groups can cultivate connections that are built on mutual respect, understanding, and trust. These bonds can enhance collaboration, promote unity, and create a sense of community among individuals who are working towards common goals. By prioritizing bonding moments in relationships, individuals can create lasting connections that enrich their lives and create a sense of belonging and connection with others.

Chapter 17: Nurturing Creativity and Imagination

- PROVIDING OPPORTUNITIES for Creativity

Providing opportunities for creativity is essential for cultivating a thriving and innovative society. Creativity is the driving force behind progress and ingenuity in all fields, from the arts to technology to business. By encouraging and fostering creativity in individuals, organizations, and communities, we can unlock the full potential of human imagination and problem-solving abilities.

One of the key ways to provide opportunities for creativity is through education. Schools and universities play a crucial role in nurturing creativity in students by offering a curriculum that emphasizes creative thinking, problem-solving, and originality. By incorporating arts, music, and other creative disciplines into the academic curriculum, students are given the space to explore their own unique talents and ideas. Additionally, educators can encourage creativity in the classroom by providing opportunities for hands-on learning, group projects, and open-ended assignments that allow students to think outside the box and express themselves in new and creative ways.

In the workplace, providing opportunities for creativity can lead to increased productivity, innovation, and job satisfaction among employees. Companies that foster a culture of creativity and experimentation are more likely to develop new products and services, solve complex problems, and adapt to changing market conditions. By encouraging employees to think creatively, take risks, and explore new ideas, organizations can stay ahead of the competition and thrive in a rapidly changing world. Employers can support creativity in the workplace by creating an open and inclusive environment where employees feel empowered to share their ideas, take risks, and experiment with new ways of working.

Beyond formal education and the workplace, communities can also play a vital role in providing opportunities for creativity. Community centers, libraries, art galleries, and other public spaces can serve as hubs for creativity and artistic expression, offering classes, workshops, and events that encourage people of all ages to explore their creative interests. By investing in cultural institutions and programs that promote creativity, communities can foster a sense of identity, belonging, and civic engagement among residents. Creativity also has the power to bring people together, bridge cultural divides, and spark dialogue and understanding among diverse groups. By nurturing creativity in individuals, organizations, and communities, we can unlock the full potential of human imagination and ingenuity. Through education, the workplace, and community engagement, we can create a culture that values and supports creativity in all its forms. By recognizing and encouraging the creative talents and ideas of all people, we can build a more vibrant, inclusive, and thriving society for the future.

- Encouraging Play and Exploration

Play and exploration are essential aspects of human development, helping individuals build skills, foster creativity, and enhance their overall well-being. Encouraging play and exploration in various environments, such as schools, workplaces, and communities, can have numerous benefits for individuals of all ages. In this discussion, we will explore the importance of play and exploration, as well as strategies for promoting these activities in different settings.

Play is often thought of as a leisure activity, but in reality, it is much more than that. Play is a vital component of learning and development, allowing individuals to practice social skills, problem-solving abilities, and creativity in a safe and enjoyable environment. Through play, children can explore their interests, experiment with new ideas, and develop their cognitive and physical abilities. In adults, play can serve as a stress-reliever, a tool for building relationships, and a way to foster innovation and productivity.

Exploration, on the other hand, involves venturing into the unknown, whether it be a new physical environment, a different perspective, or an uncharted area of knowledge. Exploration encourages individuals to step outside their comfort zones, challenge their assumptions, and expand their horizons. It can lead to deeper understanding, personal growth, and the discovery of new opportunities and solutions. By promoting exploration, individuals can develop adaptability, resilience, and a sense of curiosity that can benefit them in all aspects of their lives.

Encouraging play and exploration in various settings requires a shift in mindset and a commitment to creating environments that support these activities. In schools, educators can incorporate play-based learning activities into their curriculum, allowing students to engage in hands-on experiences that foster creativity and critical thinking. Teachers can also provide opportunities for exploration by encouraging students to ask questions, seek out information, and engage in discussions that challenge their thinking.

In workplaces, employers can create a culture that values play and exploration by providing space for employees to collaborate, experiment, and take risks. Encouraging employees to engage in activities such as team-building exercises, brainstorming sessions, and innovation challenges can help foster a sense of creativity and camaraderie within the organization. By allowing employees to explore new ideas and approaches, employers can promote innovation and problem-solving skills that can benefit the entire team.

In communities, leaders can promote play and exploration by providing access to resources and spaces that support these activities. This can include parks, playgrounds, community centers, and other recreational facilities where individuals can gather, socialize, and engage in leisure activities. By creating a supportive environment for play and exploration, communities can foster social connections, improve mental health, and promote a sense of belonging and inclusion among residents. By encouraging play and exploration in schools, workplaces, and communities, we can help individuals build skills, foster creativity, and enhance their overall well-being. Through a commitment to creating environments that support these activities, we can promote innovation, collaboration, and personal growth in all aspects of our lives. So let us embrace play and exploration as valuable tools for learning, discovery, and self-discovery.

- Supporting Artistic and Intellectual Pursuits

Supporting artistic and intellectual pursuits is crucial for cultivating a thriving and vibrant society. Artistic and intellectual pursuits not only enrich our lives personally, but also contribute to the cultural, social, and economic development of a community. By supporting artists and intellectuals, we are investing in the future of our society and fostering an environment that encourages creativity, innovation, and critical thinking.

One way to support artistic and intellectual pursuits is through funding and grants. Financial support plays a key role in enabling artists and intellectuals to pursue their passions and projects. Organizations, governments, and individuals can provide funding opportunities for artists and intellectuals to create new work, conduct research, or develop innovative ideas. By providing financial support, we are not only helping artists and intellectuals to sustain themselves financially, but also giving them the freedom and resources to fully engage in their creative and intellectual pursuits.

Another way to support artistic and intellectual pursuits is through education and mentorship. Education is essential for nurturing the next generation of artists and intellectuals. By providing access to quality education and mentorship programs, we can help aspiring artists and intellectuals to develop their skills, knowledge, and creativity. Mentors can offer valuable guidance, feedback, and support to emerging talents, helping them to navigate the challenges and opportunities of their respective fields. By investing in education and mentorship, we are promoting a culture of lifelong learning and growth that is essential for cultivating a vibrant and dynamic artistic and intellectual community.

In addition to funding and education, creating spaces and opportunities for artistic and intellectual exchange is another important way to support artistic and intellectual pursuits. Galleries, museums, theaters, libraries, and other cultural institutions play a vital role in providing a platform for artists and intellectuals to showcase their work, engage with audiences, and collaborate with one another. By promoting cultural events, exhibitions, performances, and discussions, we can bring people together to exchange ideas, inspire creativity, and foster a sense of community among artists and intellectuals. Creating a supportive and inclusive environment for artistic and intellectual exchange is essential for nurturing a thriving and diverse creative ecosystem.

Furthermore, advocating for policies and initiatives that support artistic and intellectual pursuits is crucial for ensuring the continued growth and vitality of our cultural and intellectual landscape. Governments, organizations, and individuals can play a key role in advocating for policies that promote the arts, culture, and intellectual pursuits. This includes supporting funding for arts and cultural programs, protecting intellectual property rights, and promoting diversity and inclusion in the arts and academia. By advocating for policies that support artistic and intellectual pursuits, we are not only ensuring the sustainability and growth of our creative and intellectual industries, but also affirming the value and importance of art and intellectual pursuits in our society. By providing financial support, education, mentorship, spaces for exchange, and advocating for policies that support artistic and intellectual endeavors, we can create an environment that nurtures creativity, innovation, and critical thinking. It is through our collective efforts and investments in the arts, culture, and intellectual pursuits that we can build a world that is enriched, inspired, and transformed by the creative and intellectual contributions of artists and intellectuals. Let us continue to support and celebrate the artistic and intellectual pursuits that shape and enrich our world.

Chapter 18: Coping with Life Transitions

- MOVING TO A NEW HOME

Moving to a new home can be an exciting yet overwhelming experience for many individuals. Whether you are relocating to a new city or simply moving down the street, the process of packing up your belongings and settling into a new space can be daunting. However, with proper planning and organization, the transition can be smooth and stress-free.

One of the first steps in preparing for a move is to create a timeline and checklist. Start by determining your moving date and working backwards to establish deadlines for tasks such as decluttering, packing, and hiring movers. By breaking down the process into smaller, manageable steps, you can avoid feeling overwhelmed and ensure that everything is completed on time.

Before you begin packing, it is important to declutter and organize your belongings. Take inventory of your possessions and decide what items you no longer need or want to bring to your new home. Consider donating, selling, or recycling these items to lighten your load and simplify the moving process. Not only will this help you save time and money on packing supplies, but it will also make unpacking and settling into your new home much easier.

When it comes to packing, organization is key. Start by gathering all necessary packing supplies, such as boxes, tape, bubble wrap, and markers. Clearly label each box with its contents and the room it belongs in to make unpacking a breeze. Pack heavier items in smaller boxes to prevent them from becoming too heavy to lift, and use clothing, towels, and linens to cushion fragile items. Remember to pack an essentials box with toiletries, medications, important documents, and a change of clothes for the first night in your new home.

If you are hiring professional movers, do your research and get quotes from multiple companies before making a decision. Ask for recommendations from friends and family, read online reviews, and inquire about insurance coverage and additional services. Make sure to book your movers well in advance to secure your preferred moving date and time.

In addition to packing and hiring movers, there are other important tasks to consider when moving to a new home. Notify utility companies, banks, healthcare providers, and other relevant parties of your change of address and schedule disconnection and connection dates for services. Update your address with the postal service and any subscription services you may have to ensure that you continue to receive mail at your new home.

Once you have arrived at your new home, take the time to familiarize yourself with the layout and utilities. Complete a move-in inspection with your landlord or property manager to document any existing damage or issues, and address them promptly. Unpack and set up your essentials box first, then gradually unpack and organize the rest of your belongings room by room. Take breaks as needed to avoid burnout and prioritize self-care during this transition period.

Moving to a new home can be a fresh start and an opportunity to create a space that reflects your personality and lifestyle. Embrace this new one with an open mind and a positive attitude, and allow yourself time to adjust to your new surroundings. Reach out to neighbors, join local community groups, and explore your new neighborhood to establish a sense of belonging and connection. Remember that moving is a process, and it is normal to experience a range of emotions throughout the transition. Be patient with yourself and celebrate your accomplishments as you settle into your new home.

- Welcoming a New Sibling

Welcoming a new sibling into the family is a significant and exciting milestone for everyone involved. It can be a time of joy, anticipation, and adjustment as the family grows and dynamics shift. For the older siblings, it may bring about a mix of emotions, ranging from excitement and curiosity to jealousy and apprehension. As parents, it is crucial to create a supportive and loving environment to help ease the transition for all family members and ensure a smooth integration of the new addition.

One of the most important steps in welcoming a new sibling is preparing the older children for the arrival of their new brother or sister. Communication is key in this process, as children need to feel included and informed about the upcoming changes. Parents can talk to their children about the new sibling, read books about new babies, and involve the older siblings in decision-making processes related to the baby. This can help older children feel a sense of ownership and responsibility, rather than feeling left out or ignored.

In addition to preparing the older siblings for the new arrival, parents should also take steps to prepare the physical space for the new baby. Setting up a nursery or designated area for the baby can help create a sense of anticipation and excitement for the older siblings. Involving the older children in decorating the nursery or choosing items for the baby can also help them feel more connected to the new addition. Creating a welcoming and comfortable space for the baby shows the older siblings that their needs and feelings are important as well.

As the due date approaches, parents should continue to involve the older siblings in preparations for the new baby. This can include attending doctor's appointments together, helping to choose baby names, and discussing what life will be like once the baby arrives. Encouraging older siblings to ask questions, express concerns, and share their thoughts and feelings can help them feel more prepared and involved in the process. It is essential for parents to validate the emotions of the older siblings and reassure them that their feelings are normal and okay.

Once the new baby arrives, parents should continue to support and involve the older siblings in caring for the new addition. This can include asking for their help with simple tasks, such as fetching diapers or holding the baby, and encouraging them to bond with their new sibling. Parents should also make sure to spend one-on-one time with each child to reassure them of their importance and love within the family. By prioritizing individual relationships with each child, parents can help prevent feelings of jealousy or resentment and foster a sense of unity and cooperation among siblings. By involving the older siblings in the process, creating a welcoming physical space for the new baby, and continuing to support the older siblings after the baby arrives, parents can help ease the transition and make it a positive and memorable experience for everyone involved. Providing love, patience, and understanding during this time can help strengthen family bonds and create a harmonious environment for all family members to thrive.

- Handling Divorce or Separation

Divorce or separation can be a challenging and emotional process for those involved. It is important to approach the situation with sensitivity and understanding, as each individual may experience a range of emotions and reactions during this time. It is essential to take the necessary steps to handle divorce or separation in a way that is healthy and constructive for all parties involved.

One of the first steps in handling divorce or separation is to seek support from friends, family, or a therapist. Talking to someone about your feelings and emotions can help you navigate through this challenging time and provide you with a sense of comfort and understanding. Surrounding yourself with a support network can help you feel less isolated and help you process your emotions in a healthy way.

It is crucial to prioritize self-care during a divorce or separation. This may include engaging in activities that bring you joy and relaxation, such as exercise, hobbies, or spending time with loved ones. Taking care of yourself physically, emotionally, and mentally can help you cope with the stress and emotions that come with divorce or separation. Additionally, seeking professional help from a therapist or counselor can provide you with the tools and support needed to navigate through this difficult period.

When going through a divorce or separation, it is essential to maintain open communication with your ex-partner. Establishing effective communication can help you both navigate through the legal and emotional aspects of the separation in a respectful and healthy manner. It is important to set boundaries and establish clear expectations for co-parenting or other shared responsibilities to ensure a smooth transition during this time.

Seeking legal advice and guidance is crucial when handling divorce or separation. Consulting with a family law attorney can help you understand your legal rights and options and provide you with the necessary information to make informed decisions throughout the process. A legal professional can help you navigate through complex legal issues, such as asset division, child custody, and spousal support, and ensure that your rights are protected during the divorce or separation.

It is important to seek closure and find ways to move forward after a divorce or separation. This may involve seeking closure through therapy or counseling, engaging in self-reflection, and setting new goals and priorities for yourself. Finding closure can help you heal and move on from the past in a healthy and constructive way, allowing you to embrace a new one in your life with confidence and optimism. Seeking support from friends, family, or a therapist, prioritizing self-care, maintaining open communication with your ex-partner, seeking legal advice, and seeking closure are all important steps in handling divorce or separation in a healthy and constructive manner. By taking these steps, you can navigate through this difficult time with resilience and strength, allowing you to move forward with confidence and optimism towards a brighter future.

Chapter 19: Dealing with Teenage Challenges

- COMMUNICATING WITH Teenagers

Communicating with teenagers can be a challenging task, as this demographic is often characterized by their unique developmental stage, interests, and communication preferences. Understanding how to effectively communicate with teenagers is crucial for parents, educators, and other caregivers to establish strong relationships, foster trust, and navigate potential conflicts. By recognizing the factors that influence teenage communication, implementing effective strategies, and maintaining open lines of communication, adults can better connect with teenagers and support their emotional, social, and cognitive development.

One of the key factors to consider when communicating with teenagers is their developmental stage. Adolescence is a period of rapid physical, cognitive, and emotional growth, during which teenagers are navigating their identities, relationships, and autonomy. This developmental stage is marked by increased independence, a desire for experimentation, and a tendency to question authority. Understanding these developmental changes can help adults approach communication with teenagers in a more empathetic and patient manner. Recognizing that teenagers are seeking autonomy and self-expression can help adults validate their feelings and perspectives, leading to more productive and meaningful conversations.

In addition to considering the developmental stage of teenagers, it is important to acknowledge their interests, preferences, and experiences. Teenagers are often heavily influenced by peer relationships, social media, and popular culture, which can shape their values, beliefs, and communication styles. By staying informed about current trends, technology, and cultural references, adults can better connect with teenagers and engage in conversations that are relevant and relatable. Showing genuine interest in teenagers' hobbies, passions, and concerns can help build rapport and trust, creating a foundation for open and honest communication.

Effective communication with teenagers also involves adapting communication strategies to meet their unique needs and preferences. Teenagers may respond differently to various communication styles, such as directiveness, involvement, or collaboration. Some teenagers may prefer clear instructions and boundaries, while others may appreciate more flexibility and autonomy. By recognizing individual differences and tailoring communication approaches accordingly, adults can create a safe and supportive environment for teenagers to express themselves and share their thoughts and feelings. Encouraging teenagers to take ownership of their communication style and preferences can also empower them to advocate for their needs and rights in various contexts.

Maintaining open lines of communication with teenagers is essential for building trust, resolving conflicts, and promoting positive relationships. Establishing regular opportunities for dialogue, such as family meetings, check-ins, or one-on-one conversations, can help adults stay connected with teenagers and address potential issues in a timely manner. Creating a safe and non-judgmental space for teenagers to express themselves, ask questions, and seek support can foster mutual respect and understanding. Adults can also model effective communication skills, such as active listening, empathy, and validation, to demonstrate the importance of respectful and constructive dialogue.

Effective communication with teenagers requires patience, empathy, and an ongoing commitment to building trust and understanding. By considering teenagers' developmental stage, interests, and preferences, adapting communication strategies to meet their needs, and maintaining open lines of communication, adults can navigate the challenges of teenage communication and foster positive relationships. Through meaningful and respectful interactions, adults can support teenagers' emotional, social, and cognitive development, ultimately empowering them to thrive and succeed in a complex and ever-changing world.

- Setting Boundaries and Expectations

Setting boundaries and expectations is an essential aspect of both personal and professional relationships. Boundaries are defined as the limits we set for ourselves in order to ensure healthy and respectful interactions with others. Expectations, on the other hand, refer to the standards or goals we have for ourselves and others in terms of behavior, performance, or outcomes. When boundaries and expectations are clearly communicated and understood, it can lead to more effective communication, increased productivity, and stronger relationships.

In both personal and professional settings, setting boundaries is crucial for maintaining a sense of self-respect and self-worth. Without boundaries, it is easy to become overwhelmed and lose sight of our own needs and priorities. By establishing clear boundaries, we are able to protect our time, energy, and emotions from being exploited or depleted by others. This can help prevent burnout, resentment, and conflict in our relationships. Additionally, setting boundaries can also help us define our own identity and communicate our values and priorities to others.

When it comes to expectations, having clear and realistic standards can help guide our actions and decisions. Expectations can motivate us to strive for excellence and achieve our goals. However, it is important to be mindful of setting expectations that are too high or unrealistic, as this can lead to disappointment, frustration, and feelings of failure. By setting realistic expectations for ourselves and others, we can create a sense of accountability and drive towards achieving positive outcomes. It is also important to communicate expectations clearly and openly, so that everyone involved is on the same page and working towards a common goal.

In the workplace, setting boundaries and expectations is particularly important for creating a positive and productive work environment. When employees understand their roles, responsibilities, and objectives, they are better able to focus on their work and contribute effectively to the team. Clearly defined boundaries can help prevent conflicts and misunderstandings, while realistic expectations can promote accountability and performance excellence. Managers and leaders play a crucial role in establishing and enforcing boundaries and expectations within their teams, as they set the tone for how individuals interact and collaborate with one another.

In personal relationships, setting boundaries and expectations can help promote healthy communication, respect, and mutual understanding. By clearly communicating our needs, desires, and boundaries to others, we can foster stronger connections and build trust and intimacy. It is important to be assertive in setting boundaries and not be afraid to speak up when our boundaries are being violated. Additionally, having realistic expectations for ourselves and others can prevent disappointment and frustration, and allow for more harmonious and fulfilling relationships. Ultimately, setting boundaries and expectations is about establishing healthy boundaries for ourselves and respecting the boundaries of others, while also having clear and realistic standards for behavior and performance. By establishing clear boundaries and realistic expectations, we can protect our own well-being, communicate our values and priorities to others, and promote healthy and respectful relationships. Whether in the workplace or in personal relationships, setting boundaries and expectations can lead to increased productivity, effective communication, and stronger connections with others. It is important to be mindful of our own boundaries and expectations, and to communicate them openly and assertively to those around us. Ultimately, setting boundaries and expectations is about creating a framework for positive interactions and outcomes, and promoting mutual respect, understanding, and growth.

- Helping Teens Navigate Peer Pressure

Peer pressure is a common phenomenon that many teenagers face on a daily basis. It can come in various forms, such as being pressured to engage in risky behaviors like smoking, drinking, or using drugs, or feeling the need to conform to certain standards set by their peers. As adults, it is important for us to understand the challenges that teenagers face when it comes to peer pressure and to provide them with the necessary support and guidance to navigate these pressures successfully.

One of the key factors that can help teens navigate peer pressure is to build their self-confidence and self-esteem. When teenagers have a strong sense of self-worth and believe in themselves, they are more likely to resist negative influences from their peers. Encouraging teens to develop healthy relationships with themselves and to practice self-care can help them build resilience against peer pressure. Helping teens to identify their strengths and talents, and to value themselves for who they are, can empower them to make decisions that align with their values and beliefs, rather than succumbing to external influences.

Another important aspect of helping teens navigate peer pressure is to open up lines of communication between parents, caregivers, and teenagers. It is essential for adults to create a safe and non-judgmental space for teens to express their thoughts and feelings, and to ask for help when they need it. By fostering trust and open communication, adults can better understand the challenges that teenagers face and provide them with the support they need to overcome peer pressure. Listening actively and empathetically to teens' concerns and experiences can help build a stronger bond between adults and teenagers, and empower teens to make informed decisions in the face of peer pressure.

In addition to building self-confidence and fostering open communication, it is important for adults to educate teens about the risks and consequences of giving in to peer pressure. Many teenagers may not fully understand the potential harm that certain behaviors can have on their health and well-being, and may be more inclined to go along with their peers without considering the consequences. By providing teens with accurate and age-appropriate information about the dangers of risky behaviors, adults can empower teens to make informed decisions and resist negative influences from their peers. Encouraging teens to think critically about the consequences of their actions and to consider the long-term impacts can help them navigate peer pressure more effectively.

Furthermore, adults can help teens navigate peer pressure by teaching them assertiveness skills and strategies to handle difficult situations. Many teenagers may struggle to say no to their peers or to stand up for themselves when faced with pressure to engage in risky behaviors. By providing teens with tools and techniques to assertively communicate their boundaries and to resist negative influences, adults can empower teens to assert their autonomy and make decisions that align with their values and beliefs. Encouraging teens to practice assertiveness through role-playing exercises and real-life scenarios can help them build confidence in standing up for themselves and resisting peer pressure. By providing teenagers with the necessary support and guidance to develop resilience against peer pressure, adults can empower teens to make informed decisions and resist negative influences from their peers. Through a collaborative effort between adults and teenagers, we can create a safer and more supportive environment for teens to navigate peer pressure successfully and thrive in their social interactions.

Chapter 20: Conclusion

- REFLECTING ON YOUR Parenting Journey

Reflecting on your parenting journey can be a powerful and rewarding experience. It allows you to take stock of your accomplishments and challenges, and to identify areas where you can grow and improve as a parent. Parenting is a journey that is full of ups and downs, joys and struggles, successes and failures. It's important to take the time to reflect on your experiences as a parent, to learn from them, and to use that knowledge to become a better and more effective parent.

One of the key benefits of reflecting on your parenting journey is that it can help you to better understand yourself as a parent and the impact that your parenting style has on your children. By taking the time to reflect on your actions, decisions, and interactions with your children, you can gain insight into your strengths and weaknesses as a parent. You can identify patterns of behavior that may be unhelpful or harmful to your children, and make changes to improve your parenting style.

Reflecting on your parenting journey can also help you to strengthen your bond with your children. By taking the time to reflect on your experiences as a parent, you can gain a deeper understanding of your children's needs, desires, and feelings. This increased understanding can help you to connect with your children on a deeper level, and to build a stronger and more supportive relationship with them. When children feel understood and valued by their parents, they are more likely to thrive and flourish.

Another benefit of reflecting on your parenting journey is that it can help you to identify areas where you can improve as a parent. No parent is perfect, and we all have room to grow and develop in our parenting skills. By reflecting on your experiences as a parent, you can identify areas where you may need to make changes or adjustments in order to better meet the needs of your children. This could involve setting boundaries, improving communication, or seeking support and advice from other parents or professionals.

Reflecting on your parenting journey can also help you to build resilience and cope with the challenges of parenting. Parenting can be stressful and demanding, and it's important to have strategies in place to help you navigate the inevitable ups and downs of raising children. By reflecting on your experiences as a parent, you can gain insight into the coping mechanisms that have worked well for you in the past, and identify strategies that can help you to manage stress, stay positive, and bounce back from setbacks. By taking the time to reflect on your experiences, you can gain insight into your strengths and weaknesses as a parent, build a stronger bond with your children, identify areas for improvement, and develop resilience in the face of parenting challenges. Reflecting on your parenting journey is not only beneficial for you as a parent, but also for your children, as it can help you to support their growth and development in a more effective and meaningful way. So take the time to reflect on your parenting journey, and use that knowledge to become the best parent you can be.

- Celebrating Successes and Learning from Mistakes

Celebrating successes and learning from mistakes are two essential components of personal and professional growth. When we achieve our goals and accomplish something meaningful, it is important to take the time to acknowledge and celebrate our successes. This not only boosts our self-esteem and morale but also motivates us to continue striving for excellence in our future endeavors. On the other hand, mistakes are inevitable, but they also provide valuable learning opportunities. By reflecting on our failures and understanding what went wrong, we can gain valuable insights that will help us avoid making the same mistakes in the future.

One of the reasons why celebrating successes is so important is that it helps us recognize our achievements and feel a sense of pride in our accomplishments. Whether we have met a personal goal, completed a challenging project at work, or reached a milestone in our career, taking the time to celebrate these successes can have a significant impact on our confidence and self-esteem. By acknowledging and celebrating our successes, we are able to build a positive self-image and reinforce our belief in our abilities and potential for future success.

In addition to boosting our self-esteem, celebrating successes also serves as a powerful motivator for setting and achieving new goals. When we take the time to celebrate our accomplishments, we are more likely to feel motivated and inspired to continue pushing ourselves to reach higher levels of achievement. This sense of momentum can be instrumental in fueling our drive to pursue new challenges and overcome obstacles in our personal and professional lives. By celebrating our successes, we are able to create a positive feedback loop that propels us towards even greater accomplishments in the future.

Similarly, learning from mistakes is a crucial aspect of personal and professional development. While making mistakes can be discouraging and demoralizing, it is important to remember that they also provide valuable learning opportunities. By analyzing our failures and understanding what went wrong, we can gain insights into where we went off course and how we can avoid making the same mistakes in the future. This process of reflection and self-assessment is essential for growth and improvement, as it enables us to identify areas for development and take corrective action to prevent similar errors from occurring again.

When it comes to learning from mistakes, it is important to adopt a growth mindset that embraces failure as a natural part of the learning process. Instead of viewing mistakes as a reflection of our abilities or worth, we should see them as opportunities for growth and self-improvement. By reframing our perception of failure in this way, we can approach our mistakes with a sense of curiosity and openness, using them as valuable feedback to inform our future decisions and actions. In doing so, we can leverage our failures as stepping stones towards success, rather than obstacles that hold us back.

In order to effectively learn from our mistakes, it is important to take a proactive and reflective approach to self-assessment. This involves taking the time to analyze what went wrong, identify the root causes of the mistake, and develop a plan of action to address and correct the issue. By engaging in this process of self-reflection and self-correction, we can gain valuable insights into our thought processes, behaviors, and decision-making strategies. This, in turn, enables us to develop greater self-awareness and emotional intelligence, which are essential skills for navigating the complexities of personal and professional life.

Another key aspect of learning from mistakes is seeking feedback and guidance from others. By soliciting input from mentors, colleagues, or trusted advisors, we can gain fresh perspectives and insights that can help us better understand the causes of our mistakes and identify potential solutions. Furthermore, receiving constructive feedback from others can help us develop a more objective and nuanced understanding of our strengths and weaknesses, enabling us to make more informed decisions and improvements in the future. By leveraging the collective wisdom and expertise of others, we can accelerate our learning and growth and avoid repeating the same mistakes in the future. By taking the time to acknowledge and celebrate our accomplishments, we can boost our self-esteem, motivation, and confidence, propelling us towards even greater achievements in the future. Similarly, by embracing our mistakes as valuable learning opportunities and approaching them with a growth mindset, we can gain valuable insights into our behaviors and decision-making processes. Through proactive self-reflection, seeking feedback from others, and taking corrective action, we can leverage our failures as opportunities for growth and development, ultimately paving the way for greater success and fulfillment in our personal and professional lives.

- Embracing the Ongoing Process of Parenting

Parenting is a complex and dynamic process that involves a wide range of responsibilities and challenges. It is a journey that begins before a child is even born and continues throughout their entire life. As parents, our role is to provide love, support, guidance, and discipline to help our children grow and develop into healthy, happy, and successful individuals. However, the process of parenting is not always easy or straightforward. It can be filled with ups and downs, triumphs and setbacks, joys and frustrations. Embracing the ongoing process of parenting means accepting and embracing these challenges as opportunities for growth and learning.

One of the key aspects of parenting is recognizing that it is an ongoing process that evolves and changes as our children grow and develop. What works for a toddler may not work for a teenager, and what works for one child may not work for another. As parents, we must be flexible and adaptable, willing to try new approaches, and learn from our mistakes. It is important to remember that parenting is not a one-size-fits-all endeavor. Each child is unique, with their own strengths, weaknesses, and personality traits. As such, we must be open to adjusting our parenting style to meet the individual needs of each of our children.

Another important aspect of embracing the ongoing process of parenting is being open to seeking help and support when needed. Parenting can be overwhelming and stressful at times, and it is okay to ask for help. This may involve reaching out to family members, friends, or other parents for advice and support, or seeking the guidance of a professional, such as a therapist or counselor. It is important to remember that seeking help is a sign of strength, not weakness, and that no parent has all the answers. By being willing to ask for help when needed, we can better navigate the challenges of parenting and provide the best possible care for our children.

In addition, embracing the ongoing process of parenting means prioritizing self-care and well-being. As parents, we often put our children's needs above our own, sacrificing our own health and happiness in the process. However, it is important to remember that we cannot pour from an empty cup. In order to be the best parents we can be, we must take care of ourselves physically, emotionally, and mentally. This may involve setting aside time for self-care activities, such as exercise, meditation, or hobbies, or seeking support from a therapist or counselor to address any mental health issues. By prioritizing our own well-being, we can better cope with the demands of parenting and be more present and attentive to our children's needs.

Furthermore, embracing the ongoing process of parenting means accepting and embracing the imperfections and uncertainties that come with raising children. Parenting is not a perfect science, and we will inevitably make mistakes along the way. It is important to remember that perfection is not the goal of parenting, but rather progress and growth. By acknowledging our imperfections and learning from our mistakes, we can become more compassionate, empathetic, and understanding parents. It is also important to remember that we do not have all the answers, and that it is okay to admit when we are unsure or confused. By embracing the uncertainties of parenting and being open to learning and growing, we can become more effective and confident parents. It is a process that is filled with challenges, but also opportunities for growth and learning. By recognizing that parenting is a dynamic and evolving endeavor, seeking help and support when needed, prioritizing self-care and well-being, and accepting the imperfections and uncertainties that come with raising children, we can become better, more effective parents. Parenting is not easy, but by embracing the ongoing process with an open mind and heart, we can create loving, supportive, and nurturing environments for our children to thrive and succeed.